Our Say, Not Hearsay

Our Say, Not Hearsay

Wartime Accounts from an Anglo-French community in Paris

Edited by
Grahame Warby

Mansion Field

Mansion Field
An imprint of Zeticula Ltd
The Roan,
Kilkerran,
KA19 8LS
Scotland

http://www.mansionfield.co.uk
First published in 2014
This collection © 2014 Zeticula Ltd
Cover image by Friederike Hiepko

This work is dedicated primarily to all those who contributed their accounts herein; Thank You All.

To my kind and supportive wife Diane and our wonderful son Alex ... who are my *raisons d'être*.

To my late Grandfather, Sidney William James Morris; I think he'd have been quite impressed with this initiative.

"This story shall the good man teach his son..."
William Shakespeare, *Henry V*

Acknowledgements

This book would not have been possible without the support of the following:

All of the Contributors (affectionately referred to as "the Players"), for obvious reasons.

Mr. Alec Harvey, Mr. Oliver Finegold, Miss Amy Gardner and Mr. David Franklyn (the Sub-Editors), for additional proofing, style and other useful tips and suggestions.

Mr. Gyles Longley, for his assistance with publishing contacts and other very useful advice and guidance throughout.

Mr. Roger Thorn, for his support and enthusiasm throughout, and assistance with obtaining additional accounts for this work.

Mr. Mark Yates, for his continued rallying of "the troops" in this escapade.

Mrs. Janet Warby, for her first class secretarial (typing) support, as well as assisting in the procurement of various accounts in this work. Thanks Mum.

Ms. Joan Hicks for her continued support from inception to close, and for assisting in the procurement of further accounts.

Contents

Illustrations

Preface

I am full of admiration for Grahame Warby's initiative in compiling this collection of contributions from the members and friends of the Paris Branch of The Royal British Legion. The net proceeds from all his hard work, and yours, the contributors, will be donated to the Paris Branch. On behalf of the Branch may I thank him and you for that generosity of spirit. The project is an excellent example of the Legion's motto: "Service not Self". But then Grahame is the scion of the Warby and Morris family which epitomizes service, both in uniform to the Queen and to the Legion.

We are so fortunate in the Paris Branch to enjoy the fellowship of so many French and British members with such rich experiences of those dark days of wartime. You will be humbled, as I was, when you read these accounts. They are inspiring. In a little known speech by Sir Winston Churchill, given on a private visit to his Alma Mater, Harrow School, on 29th October 1941, in those sternest of days, he said:

"Never give in, never give in,
never, never, never, never –
in nothing, great or small,
large or petty – never give in
except to convictions of honour
and good sense !"

You will find that sentiment running through these accounts which you are about to read. That gritty determination when backs are to the wall.

Winston's words are a lesson for living our lives. Read on.

Roger Thorn
Chairman of the Royal British Legion
(Paris Branch)

Introduction

I started this idea for a book about the collective experiences of some Anglo/French folk in Paris caught up in various exploits of conflict, though predominantly during World War II, some six months ago. I wanted to make a book, a collection of accounts that I knew had not been written or widely disseminated in the manner in which they ought to have been; indeed, in the manner that posterity (unwittingly) requires, whether it knows it or not.

I have been humbled, to say the least, by the "players" who have contributed and acquiesced to my slight bullying to put this book together. I am sure that at times, and to certain of these players I have been a pain in the proverbial ... And yet contribute they have.

These accounts have been brought together out of the belief that humanity, posterity, and anyone else with a similarly deserving interest, should hear them.

I have always been an avid reader of history, and the only programmes I tend to watch on television are documentaries (largely on World War II, but also on Louis XIV and contemporary British - the Stewarts - history). Indeed, my wife would be the first to say I watch too much of this - but is there too much one can observe, digest and use from history? I think not. And I am, by now, set in my ways, so the point is moot.

I have greatly enjoyed the entire process of putting this volume of material together; yet my role has remained rather administrative. You see, this is not my book: these are not my stories.

The glory, respect and recognition for this book lands squarely on those players which have so kindly and with utmost dedication, to fact and timing, shared what are very personal accounts. I thank them all for allowing me to publish the fruits of such intrusion. I am fortunate, as no doubt many who read this book will be similarly so, for I have not had to endure war on a personal level. As much as some of these accounts point to instances of bravado, camaraderie, and romance as themes (to highlight a few) which emerge from the players' experiences, I hope neither I nor anyone else should have to endure the types of conflict which feature in this book.

Originally, this book was based on a united theme in that the players who have submitted their accounts are all members of the Royal British Legion (Paris Branch) – both English and French members. Sadly, for legal branding reasons, we were required to shift the emphasis away from this affiliation. But no matter. This book is as much a collection of stories from an Anglo/French community in Paris who have lived through a shared common set of experiences as compared to the mutual affiliation they share of a notable charitable organisation. Furthermore, this is not a political book; the accounts within are personal and don't generally tend to any leaning of politics. The players who have contributed to this book have done so with magnificent support for its aims. This is not a tome for profit; any sales proceeds will be donated to the Royal British Legion (Paris Branch). I bid you to read on.

Grahame Warby

Part 1: Children and Evacuee Accounts

e·vac·u·ee

[ih-vak-yoo-ee, ih-vak-yoo-ee]

noun

a person who is withdrawn or removed from a place of danger, a disaster area, etc.

Origin:

1935–40; < French évacué, past participle of évacuer to evacuate

Being A Child In War-Time Britain - The City Boy Evacuee

Sidney William Morris

The evacuation of Britain's cities at the start of World War Two was arguably the biggest and most concentrated mass movement of civilian people in Britain's history. In the first four days of September 1939, nearly 3,000,000 people were transported from towns and cities in danger of being bombed. These were children, elderly people and pregnant women. Mostly they were children.

The year was 1940. I was nearly ten years old. I found myself with a gas mask in a cardboard box, label attached to my coat with my small suitcase, heading for the local Community Centre where, together with my younger sister, Mary, we went with our mother. My friends were also there and we boys naturally got together and tried to find out why we were all together in this centre; it was odd to say the least.

We soon found out, as one of our teachers told us, that we were being sent to the country so that we would be safe from the bombs that "Mr. Hitler" was going to drop on London to make us give in and let him take over our Country.

As my family lived in Peckham in South East London and there had been bomb damage in our area (we lived near the docks), our parents were told to make us ready for a nice journey. My mother had been sent a letter telling her to pack two vests, two under-pants, pyjamas, socks, shorts and trousers, shirts and a pullover. For the girls, it was much the same but they had dresses or shirts and skirts and cardigan. We also had to have stout walking shoes and plimsolls, or whatever our parents could afford. My grandmother, being of Irish descent, was not letting us go scruffy and duly provided what she thought was suitable.

We were lined up in the yard, with labels with our names on our coats, and marched to waiting trams to take us to Waterloo Station where we would be taken to the country on the train. The teachers who were with us kept telling us not to suck the labels. Some of the little kids were so unhappy that they had to suck on something. As we went off some of the older children started to sing *"The Lambeth Walk"* and choruses of *"Wish Me Luck as You Wave Me Goodbye"*; it was just going to be a big adventure. The only thing that worried me was that my mother was crying and saying: "Take care of your sister" and "Don't forget to write and let us know you are OK". Why would I not be OK?

We were not told where we were going, but after what seemed like an age, we arrived in Exeter. We were all taken to the local hall, much like our Community Centre - not that it was called that. People were calling out names of children and they would go to a man or lady who would take them away. My name was called and I was being sent to an elderly couple who had no children of their own. I looked to see where my sister was, only to find she was being taken by some lady who had a couple of other children with her. Mary, my sister, called for me but was told to be quiet and go with the nice lady.

The couple I was billeted with gave me my own room, and quickly took me out to buy some new clothes. My sister tells a story of how she saw me in the park one day with the nice people I was to live with. She says I had a pair of knickerbockers on with a jacket, straw hat and a cane. Now I do not remember this. She says she called out " 'ello Siddy, how you doing?" My "foster family" asked me who this little girl was and I said she was my younger sister, Mary. They went to talk to her. I do not know what was said, but shortly after we left to go back to the nice house with the green door and gate.

My foster family gave me pencils and paper to draw with and they saw that I had a knack for drawing. It was to stand me in good stead later in my life.

Mary had written to our parents in Peckham, to say she was not happy where she was. By this time my parents had two more children and the bombs were beginning to fall on London. My father was working with the rescue teams and told my mother to take the younger two down to Exeter and find a house and get my sister and myself to live all together. I was happy to see my mother, but sad to leave my foster family as they had been good to me. Mary was relieved to be with our mother and siblings as she hated her foster family.

Our father came down to Exeter when he could and family life went on as usual. That is until one day the Germans dropped bombs on Exeter and destroyed the Cathedral. No one thought they would come so far inland to bomb towns, we all thought they would hit the docks around the sea areas. Father came down on the next available train and told my mother to pack up and ship us all back to London. We had been in Exeter for about two years and by now we had another brother. Father said we might as well all be together in London and get bombed rather than be split up and bombed in Exeter. So as soon as we could, back to London we all went.

As I got older, my father would allow me to go with him to help dig out those people who had been bombed from the rubble. It was not very pleasant but my father was careful that I did not see any horrible sights. My father was also helping put out fires from the river when he was needed. Many buildings were hit by the German bombers and I learnt that some families who I had known in London and Exeter had been killed. It was a nasty experience to hear that your friends and their families had been killed.

I was cycling one day in the neighbourhood when I heard an airplane coming overhead. Now it did not sound like an RAF plane, but I looked up and horror of all horrors, I saw it was a German plane. As he saw me cycling along, he fired. I dived into the nearest ditch. That was my brush with near death; or so I thought.

The second time I faced the enemy was this time with a V1 bomb known as the "Doodlebug". This was the flying bomb that after a while cut out and just dropped anywhere. Again I was riding my bike and heard the distinctive sound of the V1. I looked up and peddled like fury to escape the bomb. Now I completely forgot what I had been told as fear overtook any sense I may have had. We were told never to run from the Doodlebug as it could not change direction. In my fear I forgot this and ran away from it! I narrowly escaped being hurt or worse, as I again jumped into a ditch. I had on some new clothes for one of my birthdays, so I got a real telling off from my parents when I went home with torn clothes. They were not amused!

Some years later, when I was married and had my own family, I suggested we go to Exeter and see if I could remember where the house I had lived in was. Luckily I did find the house, but the elderly couple that had taken me in were sadly no longer alive.

Being A Child In Wartime Britain - The Country Girl

Jean Morris

Of course, in Wartime Britain, German attacks were not purely focused on the cities of the nation – coastal and more rural areas of the land were as exposed at certain points. The following account details the impact of foreign Allied troops billeted amongst the local British people and the relative novelty of this phase of the War.

My family was from London originally. Due to my father's health, we moved to the country in 1938. This was just before the war. We lived in Laindon, Essex, just off the Arterial Road, now the A127, which is the main road between London and Southend. This was very much countryside when we lived there.

In 1939, we were told by Mr. Chamberlain that we were now at war with Germany. All the boys played at being soldiers or pilots shooting the Germans; they were the bad guys!

We had our fair share of raids and German planes coming over and strafing us with their machine guns. My mother was out walking one day with my younger sister, when a plane swooped low and let loose a round of bullets on innocent people. My mother ran like crazy to the nearest alleyway with my sister in the pushchair and crouched over her to protect her from the raid. She was shaken but thankfully not hurt. She went back to my grandmother who was living nearby and told her what had happened. Nanny was livid and would have taken on the whole German Army if she could have; she was a formidable lady.

One morning I woke to hear my parents talking about all the tents on the Arterial Road, they spread for miles and we had a small contingent nearby. Being an inquisitive child, I quickly dressed, found my friend and went to look for ourselves. There were lots of lorries and tents with soldiers and lots of netting over items, which I was told by my older brothers was camouflage so the German planes could not see what was there. I wanted to look but was told in no uncertain terms not to go near there otherwise I might be shot! That's brothers for you.

There was a mixture of British, French, Canadians and a few Americans. The British soldiers were a bit put out by the "Yanks" being here as they had plenty of money, gum, chocolate and nylons for the girls. The saying at the time about the Americans was "Over Sexed, Over Paid and Over Here". I asked my friend, who was older than me, about all the sayings that were being said; she told me quite a few that she had heard from her father and brothers. I am afraid I cannot put these into print as they are quite rude. I did say one of these sayings one day, only to find I got a clip around the ear from my mother, who said I was not to say that ever again. When I asked why, she just said "because I say so, it is not becoming of a young girl"!

The older girls loved having the soldiers around. They were given food by the British soldiers' canteen and also got the gum and nylons from the Americans. I asked one of the American soldiers why the British called them Yanks. He was about to tell me, when a pal of his said he should not tell me as I was so young – in

1944 I was 11 years of age. I did not think I was so young but they would not tell me. I found out years later!

The Headquarters (Base Camp) of the British was situated in Dunton Road, which was in a forest. Whether the forest was a sort of camouflage, we did not know but thought it was. My elder two brothers were quite happy to tell me this.

My friend and myself used to talk to a young French-Canadian soldier. We thought he was American until he told us he was from Quebec, which was French speaking – *oh la la*! He would never tell us his real name, only that we could call him "Frenchy". One day he was looking at some rosaries. I asked him what they were and he told me. He was Catholic and they carried around a rosary to pray at times. Being an Anglican, I thought this was funny, I had never seen these before. He said that he had two extra sets of rosaries and that my friend and I could choose one each. I saw he had another one which was a crystal one, so I asked if I could have that one. He said no because his sweetheart had given it to him just before he left Canada. I chose a yellow rosary and my friend chose the blue one.

There was talk that the soldiers were on the move. My dad went to see the "boys" as he called them. He took with him a rabbit hutch with two rabbits inside – we had a large garden and my father kept livestock and vegetables that way we would always have food. The soldiers asked my father what they should do with the rabbits. Father told them that wherever they were going, they may not have food, they might not have their rations. So father told them to either let the rabbits go when they got to wherever it was they were going or, if they were hungry to hit them on the back of the neck, skin them and put them in the stewpot; that way they would have food for a couple of days.

Talk around the table at home was of when the soldiers would go, something was obviously happening but no one knew what. I wanted to go and see them after dinner but father told me I could not go. The next morning, I was on my way to school and saw that the tents and soldiers had all gone. I raced back home to tell my father and mother. I asked where they had gone, but all father would say was he did not know but just hoped God would keep them safe. I was sad that I could not say goodbye to "Frenchy" and his mates. I think the soldiers were camped in Laindon for about a month. Of course we later heard about the invasion of Normandy. These brave soldiers were part of Operation Overlord.

One day after the soldiers left I lost the cross of the rosary, I don't know what happened, it just came off. I wondered if this was a way of telling me that "Frenchy" had been killed. I will never know.

I married a chap from the south of London who just so happened to be a Catholic. I showed him the rosary one day and he told me how Catholics use them. My eldest daughter has the rosary now and she found an old cross which she had connected to the rosary beads, so it is complete again.

War Memories of a Very Young Child

Muriel Langle

The following contribution brings out some very common features of what it was like to be evacuated, how the Government employed certain tones of advertising language geared towards the war effort, the use of captured POWs by the British, the depiction of the enemy in a somewhat "bogie-man" light, and the impact and effects of wartime rationing on the domestic population from a macro- to micro-economic level.

We lived in a town on the East coast which was considered dangerous, and were evacuated to a farm further inland but only stayed two weeks. Our father was a teacher so he had to stay in the town, but his school was bombed several times, perhaps because there were four buildings at each corner of a large playing field, so it looked like an airfield. He had a white tin hat with ARP painted on it, and had to go out when there was an air raid.

When we returned to the town, my brother and I would take our teddy bears under one arm and pillows under the other, and go down the garden to our air raid shelter when it was bed time. Forty years later, when selling the house, we went down into the shelter again and were amazed to see how small it was – just room for two small camp beds and a chair for our mother. The ceiling was still black from the candle smoke, and the smell took us back all those years. How our mother ever coped with two small children, hearing the bombs falling and the planes overhead, I can't think.

Very occasionally we went to Colchester by train to see our grandparents. Large posters at the station said, "Is your journey really necessary?", and there was also a poster I loved, advertising Andrews Liver Salts, with a picture of a fat man feeling in his back pocket and saying, "I must have left it behind".

One day on a walk we passed a German plane which had crashed in a field by the road. I can't remember feeling any emotion at all; my brother had made me afraid of Germans by saying, "There's a German under your bed" and "If you don't do as I say, I'll tell the Germans".

Whenever we went out, my brother and I would run ahead on returning "to see if the house is still there". Miraculously, it always was, although there were several near misses. A bungalow just round the corner had a direct hit, and the morning after that air raid there was a twisted bed on the pavement in front of our neighbour's house.

On Michaelmas Day, 1942, one of our cousins was killed when a bomb fell on his school in Petworth, in full daylight. He was 9. Although I was only four I can remember the words of the telegram our uncle sent: "poor little David killed this morning". I still have the newspaper cuttings about this in one of my scrap books.

There were no sign posts so that if the Germans landed they would not know where they were. Every evening there was the "black out", when all light had to be hidden by curtains so that enemy planes wouldn't know if they were above a town. The police patrolled, and would knock at the door if a speck of light showed through the curtains. Our windows had strips of paper stuck diagonally on the glass to stop them from shattering if a bomb fell too near. The ceilings in our house had all fallen down before the end of the war.

We lived near a road which had several roundabouts. During the war these were left in place, but a road was also built straight through them so that tanks could get to the coast quicker. Some roads had concrete blocks built across them – about one cubic metre of concrete – supposedly to stop enemy lorries should they land.

We all had gas masks in canvas cases. Like other very young children, I had a "Mickey Mouse" gas mask.

The war was still on when I started school. Sometimes there were air raids and we had to sit in the underground shelters. These were narrow and smelt of dampness, with benches each side made of narrow planks. We sang songs then; my favourite was *You are my Sunshine*. We used to knit squares to make blankets for the soldiers, and dishcloths. We were told that if we were more than halfway to school when the air raid siren sounded we should continue to school; if not halfway there we should return home. The classrooms were heated by coal fires and lit by gas lights. Every day at play-time we were given a bottle of milk to drink. The crate was put in front of the fire in winter to warm the milk. Children also had a ration of rosehip syrup which contains lots of vitamins. We used to collect rosehips in the autumn, and one year we had to collect acorns for pigs. Rationing went on until 1953 (I still have my 1953 ration book), and I think there was less food after the war than during it. One year there was a potato shortage and fish and chip shops wouldn't sell chips unless you bought fish as well. It used to be wrapped up in newspaper, and at one time you had to take your own newspapers to wrap it in.

On St George's Day every year we had to go into the playground at school and salute the flag. One of the first things I learnt was which way up the Union Jack should go, and that has stayed with me to this day. We were all very patriotic.

Even when we were very young we were allowed to go and play on the heath without adults. We were just told "not to speak to strange men", and not to go down bomb craters because you couldn't get out and might get buried by earth falling in. We used to collect pieces of shrapnel and strips of silver paper which planes dropped for some reason. The silver paper episode only lasted a short time. I think it was something to do with radar.

When the war finally ended I can't remember any explosion of joy. I think the adults were all too exhausted to feel anything, and there certainly wasn't suddenly more food, on the contrary. We used to get food parcels from an uncle in Australia – junket powder and tinned cheese remain in my mind most. The sweet shop at the corner had a display of false sweets with a notice "Will we ever see this again?" One day at school we all had to line up and an American soldier came and gave us each one sweet. I kept mine in my hot hand for ages, and it turned into a disappointing sticky mess.

It was the same with bananas and Weetabix. We had heard so much about how wonderful they were that I was deeply disappointed. I thought that bananas would be juicy, and my first Weetabix was dry and I could hardly finish it.

We didn't listen to the wireless radio very much except for the news. During the war the newsreaders used to say their names before starting, so that people would recognise their voices and would know that the BBC hadn't been taken over by Germans giving false news. Some had strong North Country accents, like Wilfred Pickles, which would be difficult to imitate. My parents were in admiration of one reader called Bruce Belfrage, who continued to read the news in spite of the fact that the BBC was hit by a bomb while he was reading.

For Christmas Day our father usually managed to find us a chicken which would be eaten hot, then cold, and finally a soup would be made with the bones. One year he couldn't get a chicken and we had rabbit.

At one time when we invited friends to tea or when we were invited out, we used to take our own sandwiches because of the food rationing. The pleasure was in eating together.

Although we only lived 12 miles from the sea, we couldn't go there during the War, or in the first years after the war because the beach had been mined. We had heard a lot about the seaside: the yellow sand, the blue sea and the sunshine, and so when I eventually got my first glimpse of the sea, peering through coils of barbed wire at the grey water and brown shingle on a bitterly cold day, I was deeply disappointed.

An aunt and uncle who had a farm had a prisoner of war working for them. They used to say they had never seen anyone work as hard as he did. But apparently he used to get drunk and one night he was run over. He hardly spoke any English and must have been very lonely.

Evacuee

Pamela Davies

In this account we see the effects the war had all across the family unit; the evacuation of children, the drafting of cousins to fight, the loss of family members (in some cases) and the celebration of those who returned.

Pamela Davies was born on April 19th 1929, in Llanbradach, Glamorgan, Wales, only daughter of William Rydell Davies and Ann Butler. At the outbreak of World War Two the Davies family lived around the Birmingham area and like most parents when the call came to put their children out of harm's way, Pamela was sent to her Uncle Herbert and Aunt Elizabeth Bailey in the small town of Ystrad Mynach, not far from Caerphilly, Wales. So Mum was an evacuee. Not much is known about Pamela's stay with her relatives, Aunty Bet (as she was known to us, her great-nieces & great-nephew) and Uncle Herbert; apart from that she had a cousin, Eric, who, like Pamela, was an only child. He joined the R.A.F. and became a wireless operator/air gunner in 78 Squadron.

Life was already hard in that small Welsh village, but even more so on Aunty Bet. I don't know when, but Uncle Herbert had passed away some time before the war, having suffered the trauma of World War One where he served in the Welsh Guards. He'd been severely gassed while in the trenches and had suffered ever since. Tragedy struck again, on May 9th 1941. Eric's plane, a Whitley T4147 'D', was shot down coming back from a mission from Bremen; neither Eric nor his companions survived. I do not remember if mum ever told us if she was present when the news came to Aunty Bet of Eric's death.

Mum and her cat.

From then on, Aunty Bet had a strong dislike for Germans or anything that linked to them. One story that I remember mum telling me about Eric was that her father, Aunty Bet's brother, had made Pam promise never to tell Aunty Bet that Eric was getting highly inebriated before and after each mission, due to the types of plane Bomber Command was sending their boys out in. Mum had another cousin in the R.A.F., Michael Carreck, he was one of the lucky few to see the end of the war. In fact he wrote a book based on his experience, *Blaze of Glory*.

Michael Carreck flew his fifty missions and was awarded the Distinguished Flying Cross. During her stay in Ty Capel, Ystrad Mynach, mum had a cat, which the story goes, never ever caught a single mouse or rat apart from on the morning when they announced that the Führer was dead; that cat came in with a rat in its mouth! In 1988, we visited one of mum's best friends in Australia where she had emigrated. It turned out that she too had been an evacuee. Mum told me one of Joan's memories: that she was in the school playground, when a German fighter plane dived on them and blazed its guns. Pamela spent the rest of World War Two in Ystrad Mynach.

The only known picture of the Bailey family together.

Evacuee to Serviceman

Norman Shotton

Submitted by members of Norman Shotton's family, this account details one man's dogged determination to join the armed forces at all costs and join the fight – a quite common attitude prevalent among the youth of many Allied Powers' countrymen during the Second World War. Equally common was the need sometimes for those attempting to enlist to dupe would-be recruiters.

Norman Shotton was born on May 4th 1925 in Eastleigh, Hampshire, England. He was one of two sons of Bernard Louis Shotton and his wife, born Nellie May Austin. Returning home on September 3rd 1939, from a summer vacation in France, Dad was immediately evacuated to a relative in Bournemouth. While he was in Taunton's school, then in Bournemouth, he joined what was then the Air Defence Cadet Corps, later to become the Air Training Corps (A.T.C.). Before the war the family was living in Eastleigh near the local aerodrome, where the first Spitfires were test-flown. Norman was inspired to volunteer to join the R.A.F.

The first time he tried was in 1941, when he applied for a six-month University short course for potential aircrew officer cadets, putting his age up by a year. He was scuppered when the Aircrew Selection Board at the Air Ministry asked to see his birth certificate.

The alternate way in was by direct entry through the local R.A.F. recruiting office, so Norman applied a second time, altering his birth certificate to show he was a year older. His Dad was very cross and insisted he went back to recover the forged document. They had not been duped, the recruiting Sergeant said, "Come back again next year son, the war will still be on."

On the third try in 1942, Norman's dream was broken when the Medical Officer informed him that he was colour-blind. The colour vision test is very cunning. It consists of a book with, on each page, a circle made up of coloured dots, some of which are a slightly different colour from the background, making figures, letters, or designs. A person suffering from a colour vision defect sees a different pattern from that seen by someone with normal vision. Norman did not believe him, so the M.O. called in a passing W.A.A.F. and showed her the same test. To Norman's amazement she saw different things from him.

Norman in R.A.C. Uniform

For the fourth attempt he got hold of the test book, a copy of which was kept in his A.T.C. squadron office and tried to memorize the test cards but the M.O. flipped the cards a bit faster than usual, which confused Norman. When it came to the coloured lights test, it was all over!

At that time, the army was also running six-month University short courses for potential officer cadets so Norman applied and was offered a place at Kings College Newcastle where he finished top of his class.

Basic infantry training at the Rifle Brigade Depot in York was followed by further basic training at the Royal Armoured Corps Depot at Bovington, then pre-OCTU at Blackdown, and OCTU at Sandhurst from where he was commissioned into the R.A.C. on 4th November, 1944.

In early March 1945 he was posted to Italy in the Central Mediterranean Forces and joined his first service regiment, 4 Recce, in Greece, where he stayed until the Reconnaissance Corps was disbanded in 1946.

Then followed service in a number of units, all destined for disbanding, as by that time the army was being seriously run down. He was finally demobbed in the summer of 1947.

During his 5 years army service he never fired a shot in anger. He was lucky!

Norman (far right) in the Air Training Corps

A Young Girl's War Memories

Ilona Wicker

The following account details the life of a small family constantly shifting from one abode to another as prompted by the changing shape of the war. With every move from place to place came a new array of experiences to a young girl during the War.

When I was asked to write my memories of the war (1939-1945, I hasten to add), I wondered how I might organise them suitably. Actually, they can be put quite easily into 3 phases, 1939-40, 1940-42 and 1942-45.

Phase 1:

This was when I was still living, oh so happily, in the lovely home where I was born in Surrey. We had a large house and garden and life was idyllic. I'm rather ashamed to admit that the summer of 1940 was one of the happiest I'd yet had. Instead of being whisked off to enjoy an idyllic holiday in Cannes, as in previous years, we stayed at home and I had a glorious time of never-before-experienced liberty. My governess (at ten years old, I was considered too old to have a nanny) had gone home to Switzerland and all my friends were likewise free.

Our mothers were busy helping in the local Red Cross, our fathers were in the army or, like mine, working in London, and we were left to our own devices to ride around on our bikes and enjoy our unaccustomed freedom. During the frequent air-raids we would gather outside and watch breathlessly the planes fighting in the skies above: we were right in the middle of the Battle of Britain, until we were dragged indoors by our gardeners or housemaids. It was so exciting! My father, who was too old to be in the army (as he was in the front line in the Great War of 1914-18) was in the local A.R.P. (Air Raid Precaution) unit. I regularly cycled along to the wardens' post with tea and sandwiches for him and his pals, and was always welcomed boisterously.

Phase 2:

One memory that stays with me – it was a lovely summer's evening in 1940 and I was in the garden and said to my father: "Look Daddy, the sun is setting in the wrong direction, it should be over there"! And he answered: "That's not the sunset, it's the London Docks on fire". They were over 20 miles away.

Then one night in September 1940, a large bomb was dropped on our house. Luckily it was a large house, and some of it still remained, but most of it was scattered around the equally large garden. My parents and I were in our comfortably equipped air-raid shelter – but what a wreck we saw when we came to the surface next morning. My father immediately packed me and my mother off to Wales, saying "Don't be too sad, you'll be back here one day", but I knew instinctively that we wouldn't. And we never lived there again. My father died suddenly in 1942, and my mother and I moved to live in London.

That was like being in the front line, after the calm of rural Wales. We were in a top floor flat, right on Hyde Park, and we were shaken to bits not only by the bombs but by the enormous anti-aircraft guns just across the road. But I enjoyed living in London, it was quite safe in those days (apart from the raids) for a young girl to wonder around on her own, and I would sit down with my sketchbook and draw scenes of wartime life. When we were first living there my mother and I would go to a local air-raid shelter when the sirens went off, but very soon we decided to risk staying at home. The shelters were overcrowded and stuffy and home was much to be preferred.

Phase 3:

When America came into the war my mother joined the U.S. Red Cross, and so we had lots of Americans who came to be entertained *"chez nous"*. In the school holidays I would go and stay in Wales, where my grandparents had installed themselves to escape the bombs, and they remained there till the war ended. I would take myself off and sketch the areas around us. One such sketch was of an Italian Prisoner of War Camp. I would sit for hours sketching the buildings and people in them.

Throughout the war I had aircraft recognition leaflets pinned up around my bedroom. I was mad about airplanes and would have loved to have been in the R.A.F., but I was too young even for the Women's Auxiliary Air Force (W.A.A.F.). The nearest I got was when a German airplane was shot down in our garden in 1940. The wreckage was all around me, and I was thrilled when my father gave me some pieces of the fuselage to keep as a souvenir. What things one treasures as a child!

Sketch of the Italian P.O.W camp, by Ilona Wicker.

My Childhood War Recollections

Eugéne James Dagbert

When France was occupied by the Germans in 1940, a frenzied period ensued for many who attempted to leave the occupied North of France to the unoccupied Southern (or Vichy) controlled area. The area was rife with refugees, displaced persons, civilians and soldiers (many of whom were to be disbanded following the armistice) alike. From this point on, all of France entered a new era of foreign occupation or otherwise indirect control, and the national population could only wait for liberation to come some four years later.

When the armistice in Paris was signed in June 1940, I was not quite 14 years old. My English mother, my sister (17 months old) and I left Paris in early May for a small village in the Yonne (some 30 kms from Auxerre), where some friends had a house and where my father thought we would be safer. My father remained in Paris throughout as he had a war-reserved occupation.

Like everywhere else in France at that time, thousands of exhausted soldiers and civilian refugees passed through the village looking for food and shelter. It was a pitiful sight as some had been walking for days.

The village was typical of the back of beyond, even at the best of times. But with no newspapers, no mail, no reliable wireless or telephone, we were literally cut off from the rest of the world. All we knew was what passing refugees told us, which was sometimes alarming, sometimes contradictory and always unreliable. It was obvious that the whole country was on the verge of collapsing.

A small troop of Germans arrived by motorbikes, soon followed by personnel carriers, and occupied the village, requisitioning houses for their lodging. Few of them spoke French and conversation was obviously a muddle of German and French. One evening a lone German soldier came to our house and started a conversation with us in French. My mother seized the opportunity to check whether the rumoured invasion of the UK was well founded. He confirmed that an invasion was imminent, which would of course be successful due to the superiority of the German army, air force and navy. My mother did push her luck somewhat by insisting for more details, but she did not press him further as it was not clear why this soldier had picked on us to engage in conversation.

Those French soldiers with arms were disarmed and the Germans forced them to smash the butts of their rifles against the village green trees. The Germans then marched them away as POWs. Some did however, after much hesitation, manage to dress up in civilian clothes and then disappeared, albeit, to face mixed fortunes.

My mother had served as a Voluntary Aid Detachment (V.A.D.) in France in World War I, and knew the reputation of the German army in Belgium and Northern France, so decided to dress me up as a girl and put me to bed pretending that I was ill. This served no useful purpose, since no German soldier came into the house, but one of them did steal my bicycle, much to my distress.

Unknown to us, my father left Paris by car via the Porte d'Orléans just as the Germans were entering the city by the Porte de la Chapelle. He made it to Tours from where, in early September, armed with an Ausweiss [identity card] (real or false?), he arrived by car to our complete surprise, as we had received no news of him for some two months.

We then drove back to our home in Paris, being stopped only once by the Feldgendarmerie a few miles north of Fontainebleau. They checked the Ausweiss but made no comment, much to our relief, and from then on it was easy driving all the way.

Paris was almost deserted as most of the population had fled ahead of the advancing Germans, and had not yet returned. Most had their shutters closed and only very few shops were open.

Without being told, I systematically called at any shop that was open and bought in each one small quantities of basic supplies (sugar, tea, jam, soap etc.) so as to avoid the shopkeeper guessing that I was hoarding. I was, by instinct, stocking up for lean times ahead.

A short time later and unknown to me at first, my father joined a very small group who aimed to gather information about occupied France and pass it onto London. In due course it became known as Conférie Notre Dame (C.N.D.) founded by Gilbert Renault, later known as "Colonel Rémy". During his trips to the UK he was usually met at Tempford or Tangmere by Lt. Commander John Gentry.

In those early days contact with London was mainly by radio using rather cumbersome equipment. It was only later on that improved and lighter equipment and sophisticated means were made available.

My bedroom was used to send radio messages while I was at school. However, I soon realised that something was going on as my room often smelt of English cigarettes! In fact, one day I found a packet of ten Players Navy Cut which one of the operators had brought back from London. This was the start of a long-lasting smoking addiction! I was by now fully aware of what was going on in my room, but knew nothing of my father's Resistance activity outside our home.

On one occasion when I was home from school the anxiety level went up. The operator was having problems and had no other option than to send me to ask a C.N.D. wireless expert, who happened to live close by, to come over and sort things out.

In the middle of all this activity, English soldiers called on us in 1941 on their way back to the UK. They had been picked up in Calais by my father's brother, a French Police Inspector, who sheltered them by moving them from cellars, attics and other safe-houses, until reliable escape routes could be organised. They made it back to the UK and after the war they visited Calais with their families.

During the first quarter of 1942 things got tough. Robert Delatre (Bob), one of the original operators, was trailed by the Germans and urgently needed a safe place to stay. My mother asked a very poor and elderly English lady, the widow of a Frenchman, and unaware of our activities, if she "would do something for England". The answer was immediate: "Yes, of course". Bob stayed with her until he was later arrested at the Gare du Nord.

By mid 1942 most of the original C.N.D. team was wiped out. However, a new team was organised and operated until the end of the war, albeit with much more sophisticated help and equipment.

When my father was arrested on May 26th 1942, the Gestapo failed to find the transmitter and lamps, etc., which were hidden in my room. After they left, I waited for what I thought was a reasonable, if not necessarily safe, time before going out to throw the equipment into the Seine from the Neuilly end of the Pont de Courbevoie.

I was lucky because, as I reached the parapet of the bridge, a sudden heavy rainstorm meant that there was nobody around. It seemed ages before I saw the equipment hit the water. So far I had acted spontaneously, thinking of nothing else but to get rid of the evidence. Having done this, getting on my bike, I realised that my legs were like rubber and had difficulty in pushing on the pedals of my bicycle on my way home. (I had been given a replacement bike for the one stolen by the German soldier).

August 1942 saw the Dieppe raid but its short-term effect was a disappointment of course, and we had to wait almost two long years for D-Day and all that entailed. When Paris was finally liberated in August 1944, the three of us were of course relieved like everybody else, but not so jubilant.

The results of C.N.D. activities were, among others:

to hold up in Brest the powerful German warships *Scharnhorst, Gneisenau* and *Prinz Eugen,* until February 1942;

to enable the very first successful combined operation at Bruneval during the night of February 27/28, 1942; and

to provide actual maps and details of the famous Atlantic Wall installations.

The above events have of course been written up extensively over the years. My contribution is limited to a few anecdotes which, by nature, never make the headlines.

War for a Two-and-a-Half Year Old

Ian Parker

What follows is the account derived from vivid memories of a toddler during the War, his trip to Canada, and subsequent return to Great Britain. This is a very charming and alternative view of a youngster growing up in wartime.

My first memory is of a piggy back ride on my favourite aunt Maud whom, separated by an ocean, I was never to see again before she died in the height of the London blitz. In letters she told quaint tales of the City the morning after a raid, as she made it to her office from Hounslow - destruction everywhere.

She told of old gentlemen preparing for a night in the underground, winding up their watches beside them and going to sleep.

My next memory is of the ship to Canada – my mother had left me in charge of my baby sister. I abandoned my charge to look for my mother and found her chatting up a sailor - at least that was what I thought!

The snow in Canada was great fun; we seemed to have such suitable clothes. My mother dreaded the silent days. I fell in love with a pedal car and have loved them ever since. Summers on Stoney Lake were magical - I adored the boats.

As we were about to return in the summer of 1942, I remember wondering what my father could look like

– my imagined picture was nothing like him. What I remember is a very warm personality as he and his mother welcomed us, exhausted, to our house in Claygate with an open fire glowing in the hall.

War soon heated up: I was awaken to seek shelter under the stairs as the sky glowed with lights and I wondered if Hitler could be seen up there – just out of curiosity! The flying bombs and V2s were great fun for little boys – we swapped shrapnel and lurid tales of what we had seen or rather heard the day before.

I remember thinking the war would soon be over after Hess's arrival and Mussolini's capture - the just side always was bound to win.

Finally VE day came. My father would not allow us to join in the celebrations and the day Japan fell I thought the sky lit up. My father said this meant the end of warfare for fifty years.

Part 2: Civilian Accounts

ci·vil·ian
[si-vil-yuhn]

noun

1.
a person who is not on active duty with a military, naval, police, or fire fighting organization.

Origin:
1350–1400; Middle English: student of civil law < Old French civilien;

At Last They Are Together!

Silvana Gillespie

The following is an account first published in the early 1960s by Mrs. John Gillespie, an Italian lady who married an RAF airman shortly after the War in 1946. Italy of course endured much hardship during the War, particularly after the switch from allegiance to Germany and its Axis allies to the downfall of the fascist regime of Benito Mussolini. This account largely occupies this period and its effects on the local Italian population. Mrs. Gillespie details here her memories as they came flooding back to her upon returning to her familial town of Riccione after the War.

As I stood there in front of the Vannoni family tomb in the little cemetery of Riccione, memories of that Summer of 1944 when the two great Armies were locked in combat, only a few miles away, crowded my mind. I remembered the people preparing for their exodus into the safety of the countryside; I remembered our own move to Coriano and the excitement of an impending adventure; I remembered my mother's secret tears on leaving her beautiful home behind, and my father's gentle persuasion that it was sensible and wise to accept Pietro's kind invitation to go and stay with the Vannoni family at their brick factory in the country "until such time as Riccione was occupied by the Allies".

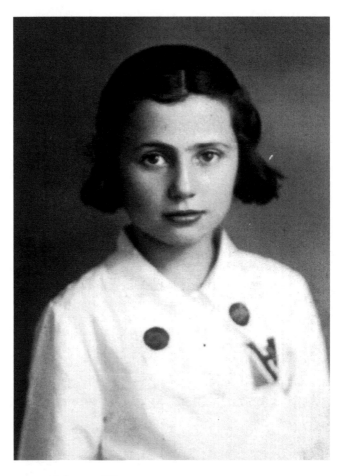

A young girl, pre-War

Going back yet further with my memories, I remembered that my young sister and I had often been guests of the family and used to sit for hours at the foot of the tall chimney watching the busy antics of the brick makers with their whining trucks and rickety old carts. We loved having games with the chimney, which seemed, in our childhood fantasy, to be like an old gentleman puffing contentedly at his pipe. How lofty and majestic it was, we could never hide from it, no matter how far into the fields we ran.

Pietro Vannoni was a fine old gentleman. He had built this thriving business and had managed it very successfully with the aid of his sons and his flock of faithful workers. The men loved and respected him, and he took a personal interest in each one of them and their families. I would often listen to stories of how, as a young man, he had been disowned by his wealthy parents for marrying without their consent. When traces of old age and the strain of a rigorous life were beginning to show on their faces, the tender devotion for each other was still very much in evidence. What a perfectly admirable family they made with their seven children.

I remembered that when we arrived at the brick factory the place looked disturbingly strange and unfamiliar: the yard empty and silent, our old friend the chimney lifeless and abandoned. The men, as we soon learned, had all set off for the fields to prepare shelters for our safety. My sister and I put down our luggage and hurried off to find them. In charge of the operation was Gino, Pietro's second eldest son: he was the most handsome, the gayest, the most appalling teaser we knew and we loved him very dearly. He was thirty-years-old, had been a prisoner of war in Russia, had managed to come back, considerably thinner and aged, but (if possible) more exuberant than over. By the way Pietro kept looking at him one would have thought that he wanted to reassure himself that his son was truly home. Gino would then put his arm around the old man's shoulder and exclaim: "It's great to be together again, Pop!"

About a week after our arrival, the Germans came. Hundreds of them swept down the hill early one morning, streaming down on their motor-bikes, troop-carriers and lorries filling the still air with loud foreign sounds. Barely awake, we watched them silently from indoors. It became apparent that they had come to stay.

As they busily began to unload, we became aware of more and more weighty sacks being carried out of the trucks with the equipment. What could they be?

As Pietro was leaving the house to approach this rowdy gathering, a staff car drew up in front of him and a distinguished looking German officer alighted from it. He called us all into the yard seemingly to inspect each one of us as we came through. I had studied German for some years at school and was the only person there capable of translating his message, which was crisp, concise and to the point. He intended to requisition the house as his headquarters, demanded good behaviour, in return for which none of us would be harmed, and wanted all the fit men in the factory to go and help his soldiers to destroy bridges and roads before the advance of the "enemy".

The unloading of the heavy sacks continued as our men were driven off in the emptied lorries. Then the Captain and his officers sat around a table with large maps opened in front of them; every so often a messenger would draw up on his motorcycle by the small group of officers and deliver his dispatches, whilst the solemn faces would once more pour over the big charts and engage in serious discussions.

Three days after the German arrival, the Captain announced in his matter of fact way, that the chimney should be destroyed as a landmark; it would be too valuable to the enemy. He made it quite clear that his decision was to be considered final and that he did not wish to argue the point. "Please inform Signor Vannoni at once!" he ordered. It took me some time to find Pietro. Eventually I saw him crossing the yard, his old head bowed, his hands clasped behind his back. How could I tell this gentle old soul that the pride of his factory was to be ruthlessly shattered? Why did such a cruel blow have to be dealt to one so blameless? I could not bring myself to tell him, my words were garbled and incoherent. With a quiet sadness in his eyes, at the end it was he who said the words; "My chimney is to come down, is it not?"

Soon everything was ready for the demolition; the dynamite placed under the chimney, the sappers under cover, us lying flat on the ground breathlessly awaiting the explosion. An eternity seemed to pass; then it came with devastating force, its roar awakening the whole countryside. When we looked up an unfamiliar gap had opened exposing the green hills beyond. A cloud of dust hung heavily over the site and, as it slowly cleared away, it revealed a mound of rubble where the magnificent monster had once so proudly stood. The old man hobbled silently away, his wife at his heels; her withered face had aged perceptibly since the arrival of the Germans. An air of sadness weighed upon the house for a few days.

My sad memories were suddenly interrupted as the figure of Nikita, a Russian orderly, floated through my mind and I could not help chuckling to myself. He looked almost grotesque in his cast-off German uniform several sizes too large for him. He had a passion for bicycles; he could not leave them alone, but alas, he could not ride them either and he was desperate to learn. Spurning all offers of help, and with a lusty look in his eyes, he would leap on the bike as if trying to overpower a wild steer, and amid a flurry of legs and pedals come almighty croppers! But was he to be deterred? With fresh determination and the most colourful set of Russian syllables he could muster, he would repeatedly pick himself up and try again, quite oblivious of our giggles in the background. On one occasion, when a wall got in his way, our amusement gave way to a dash for shelter as he rushed toward us waving his fist.

I remembered the hasty departure of the Germans. The bustle started one early afternoon amid a flurry of packing, shouting and revving of engines and it took until dark before the last lorry had departed. As night drew on, a gale blew up; its ominous wailing banishing us to the greater safety and comfort of the house. Heavy thunderclouds began to loom in the west advancing towards us with startling rapidity. Our exultation at being free of the Germans at last, was suddenly shattered by the appearance of Nikita and another German soldier at the door of the warehouse. We looked at each other questioningly. Had they been forgotten? Could it be that they were deserting? Neither of these explanations were true: Nikita had, in fact, been left behind to set fire to those mysterious sacks in the warehouse whose contents had haunted our curiosity for so many weeks. They held flour! And to think that we had, all been on the edge of starvation for so long! This caused a tremendous stir, soon to be followed by cries of protest from the workmen who pressed close, looking fierce and hostile. "He would not burn the flour!", they shouted. Besides, the chances were that the fire might spread throughout the whole surroundings on such a windy night.

Pietro commanded them to keep calm. He wanted no violence. Perhaps we could appeal to Nikita's better nature. I practically went down on my knees pleading with Nikita. Was he relenting just a little? I shall never know. He had put down the can of petrol to adjust the rifle on his shoulder. When he bent down to pick it up, it had gone! All hell let loose! Foaming at the mouth he yelled that he would shoot us all unless we produced the petrol, and he meant it! Panic-stricken, we searched frantically, groping around in the dark in a desperate attempt to find it. It was hopeless. Some of the wives shouted to their husbands to own up, not to be such fools, but their voices were drowned in the wind. The young children were crying. The old women were invoking Holy Providence. It all seemed like a bad dream. A shell exploded a few yards away scattering our pathetic little group; bits of masonry fell all around us. When we recovered from the shock, Nikita and his friend had vanished into the night. The flour was safe!

That shell was the first of many heralding the tremendous battle for Coriano which was soon to follow. The time had come for us to use the tunnel: it was cold, damp, constricted and musty, but safe. Eighteen of us spent a whole week in that dank and unsanitary hole, suffering from dirt, cramp, hunger and vermin whilst the battle raged around us.

During this awful week, Gino had been an inspiration to us all. He had on numerous occasions braved the inferno running back and forth between the house and the refuge, bringing water and what food he could find. Came the day when he excitedly crawled into the shelter crying that he had spotted Allied tanks in the field across the river. He was going back to wash and change his clothes to greet the "Inglesi". I begged my parents to let me go back with him and have a look. A few others, in their excitement, came with us, and we raced our way to the house, through the shell fire, which was too close for comfort. From the loft I had my first look at tanks; in the distance they looked like toys. It would only be a matter of hours; we set to preparing our white flags. Those of us who were in the house decided to stay there.

Unbelievably, Gino true to his word, appeared amongst us freshly shaven, clean and handsome. It was our turn to tease him! In his usual restless manner he went out laughing heartily at our affectionate leg-pulling. Minutes later, he was dragged in ashen pale with a shrapnel wound in his side.

I shall never forget his parents' expressions as he was laid gently on the bed, we mutely watched struck with horror and grief. He started to bleed from the mouth. His mother let out a scream of anguish, then everybody started to talk at once. Through the confusion l heard the mention of a German Red Cross unit over the bridge. Followed by my parents' horrified looks, I blindly ran out of the house, up the slope, over the bridge and reached the road, but there was no sign of an ambulance, instead a solitary German soldier was operating a field transmitter. I poured out my story begging him to help. Recovering from the astonishment to see a civilian there, he promised to do what he could, but as for a hospital, that was out of the question – the nearest hospital was in enemy hands. I slithered back down the slope feeling that there was a glimmer of hope. Gino had worsened considerably; my message did not seem to make any impression. His mother sat by his bed motionless and silent, unchecked tears streamed down her cheeks. Her husband paced the floor continuously rubbing his forehead as if to brush away the horrible nightmare. The others stood by. I looked questioningly at my parents and they shook their heads. Was there so little time left? I prayed fervently that the German soldier would arrive soon. He arrived at dusk with two other soldiers but not on a mission of mercy, instead to clear us out of the house. He barely glanced at the figure on the bed as he ordered us to leave. A piteous cry from Gino's mother went up: "What about my son?". "Take him with you!" he said unfeelingly. Not believing that anyone could be so cruel and deceitful I implored him to let us stay here at least, but all in vain!

Desperately our men prepared a make-shift stretcher, carefully laid Gino on it and escorted by the three soldiers, we were told to get out. Our orders were to head away from the battle area as quickly as possible or we would be shot. Accompanied by the fury of shells coming from all directions, our procession walked on.

I felt someone slipping a coin into my hands, it was one of the German guards; in the daylight I discovered it was a medal of the Virgin Mary. When we stopped at a mill for shelter and a rest some hours later, Gino was dead. His mother was still clutching in her hands a large bottle of milk in case he would be thirsty. Standing there in front of the tomb my blurred eyes could barely distinguish their three names that leaping and dancing seemed to come towards me, merging into one.

Silvana Gillespie (right), pre-war, in the young Fascist uniform of pre-war Italian schoolchildren

World War II 1939 - 1944 Vittel Camp

Joan Margaret Hicks

In this account we see a family which saw itself separated as a result of the German invasion in France. As enemy aliens, Joan Hicks and her mother were interned in camps, her brother and father arrested and similarly interned. Although conditions were better than in some camps during the war, it was to prove some time until liberation of the camps and the subsequent reunion of the family.

In June 1940, France was invaded by the German army and Paris was quickly occupied by the Gestapo. Many British families who lived in France, because of the father's job, were not able to get away in time and were therefore blocked in their homes. This was the case for our family. In no time my father and my eldest brother were arrested and put into Fresnes prison as early as October, 1940. In less than 20 minutes they were taken away!

My mother and I (only 13 at the time) were taken away the following month imprisoned in Besançon military barracks (in the east of France). Later in 1941 they captured my two younger brothers, who were 18 and 16; they were sent to the camp in the north of Paris where all British men were kept prisoners. My father and eldest brother were then transferred from the prison to this internment camp.

Three years went by, during which my eldest brother, George, escaped and managed to reach Lyon, which was in the non-occupied part of France. He became a member of the resistance and as he was speaking fluent French and English, his Chief informed him that Mr. Buckmaster of the Special Operations Executive (S.O.E.), had decided that he should remain in France to train new resistance members.

As for us, we had to wait until 1944 when the Germans decided to unite families so my father and brothers were transferred from St. Denis camp to our Vittel camp. What a joy it was to be reunited after three years of separation and hardly any news. We were in different buildings, but could see each other during the day.

In Vittel camp, British and Americans from all over Europe were concentrated. At the end of the war we were around 4,000 internees in the Vittel camp.

In Vittel camp the internees were not well informed of how the allies were advancing on the French soil. We had heard of the Overland landing, to our great joy. However, thanks to information given to us by French workers who did come into the camp for various jobs, we had heard of the Liberation of Paris and that the allied forces were making progress and surely advancing towards the east of France, where our camp was situated.

How impatient we were! During the first week of September 1944, German troops were retiring to Germany, passing along our camp. They no longer had this triumphant way of walking which they had when walking up the Champs Elysées in Paris when they invaded France.

One morning we noted the absence of the guards; the Commandant in charge of the camp and his staff had silently gone during the night without bothering to say goodbye to us!

Some experienced British men created a Committee to take care of so many internees and organise our lives. This Committee managed to get in touch with the regional Free French. We were ordered not to go out of the camp because routed German troops going through Vittel were fighting in the streets with the French Resistance. We could hear the explosions of grenades, and the smack of machine guns and explosions of bombs.

Injured Free French and German soldiers were brought into our camp where we had a small hospital where a French and British military surgeon were operating, having been brought from Prisoner of War camps from Germany to our camp, to care for internees helped by many British interned nuns. Those injured soldiers were looked after by this team, which was assisted by some volunteers, I had the honour to be one of them. Although only 16 by now, with no medical training, there I was feeling rather nervous. My first patient was a young German injured soldier, only 14 years old; he had lied about his age to enable him to fight for his country! He had received heavy shots in his bottom and was suffering. He was crying and calling for his "Mütter". I also had to deal with very young French resistance members who had run over mines and were very badly injured. They did not cry nor call for their mothers, but they kept saying "please treat us well and quickly so that we can go back and fight the Germans out of our country".

Not to be allowed to get out of the camp, although there were no longer any German guards, was hard to accept after four years of internment. One wished to enjoy freedom as soon as possible. This freedom was offered to us by General Leclerc and his men of the 2ème D.B (Division Blindée).

Early on the morning of the 12th September 1944, we were awaken by the sound of strong detonations, fairly regular and getting stronger and stronger, closer and closer. Live shells were passing over our camp, directed to fall on one hotel just outside our camp, which was occupied by convalescing German soldiers and officers.

We were asked to run down to the cellars of our respective barracks (hotels). My brothers and myself wisely obeyed and ran down to the cellars of the Grand Hotel, which was the nearest. But half way down we turned back by another staircase and climbed the staircase to the roof of that big hotel.

What a great surprise in front of our eyes. This sight is still very clear, after 60 years, in my eyes.

Coming out of the woods surrounding Vittel, we saw many tanks running down the fields, followed by Infantry men. We could easily see the firing from the guns; some of the shrapnel was passing just over our heads. I then heard my younger brother Bob, say "If our mother knew where we were, the army would not be enough to calm her down"!

Then the tanks and soldiers disappeared from our view, so we ran down, all excited, and met with many internees who were all running towards the gate of the camp. All internees were in a great state of excitement. Some were dancing, others singing, the eldest were crying with emotion. So the long waiting time was to end; freedom was at our door.

We were all pressed against the barbed wire so we could see the main street, we could hear the noise made by the tanks, we suddenly caught sight of part of a truck, then part of a tank and suddenly the whole tank followed by the soldiers with guns ready to fire. Other tanks followed. They stopped. A huge silence occurred - we just could not believe what we were seeing. We thought they were G.I.s. "Bravo" and "Hurrah" were shouted all over the camp.

What a surprise we had when we discovered that these soldiers were speaking French and were part of the

2ème Division Leclerc. We all sang *"La Marseillaise"* with an emotion rarely felt, followed by *"God Save The King"*.

Through the barbed wire we were shaking these soldier's hands and arms; some managed to kiss them. They were quite surprised to find an Internment Camp. They thought that it was a German Military Camp.

We still had a surprise to come. Towards the end of this astonishing day, we saw a jeep enter our camp; an Officer with his cane under his arm, was standing up in the jeep. We discovered that it was a General, as we looked closer we realised it was General Leclerc himself. There was an immediate hush all around.

Then General Leclerc saluted and spoke to us all.

"Je vous dois une visite. L'Angleterre nous a offert l'hospitalitié en 1940 et nous a généreusement soutenue. L'Amérique nous a donné des armes et combat sur notre sol. Je suis heureux qu'il soit donné à un Général Français de vous rendre la liberté."

("I owe you a visit. England gave us hospitality in 1940 and generously supported us. America gave us weapons and fight on our soil. I'm glad that it's a French General giving you your freedom").

His words are still in my head to this day. General Leclerc saluted and rejoined his troops. The American Military along with Leclerc organised our liberation. Some of us were taken care of by retired nurses in their own residence. To sleep in a proper bed with immaculate sheets and pillowcases was heaven! It was so comfortable that I did not sleep too well. And in the morning we had tea in bed followed by a good old English breakfast.

It took a few days before we could be definitely liberated and able to reach our family. It all started when I was 13 and a half and I was finally liberated at the age of nearly 18. Lots of sad memories, but we were young enough to enter a new life. We experienced the bombing by V1 and V2 rockets but... WE WERE FREE. We managed to get our family to England by the time the end of the war was announced. I was amongst the huge crowd in London to celebrate this great event.

Special Delivery

Marguerite Bopp

A brief but nevertheless useful insight into the constant blitz upon London by the Luftwaffe. This account demonstrates the lengths that some of those who were imprisoned and forced to work by the Germans, would go to in order to sabotage the German war effort.

In those dark times the bombs fell on London from dusk till dawn. There were few real air raid shelters and most houses had only a basement or a cupboard under the stairs. Most Londoners, when the sirens sounded, headed for the underground stations where the platforms were transformed into dormitories, long rows of bunk beds being lowered into place every evening. There, at least, there was company.

Our station was Clapham Common and my mother took me there each evening. The platforms were crowded with people and every new arrival would hunt out their own group of friends and neighbours before slowly settling down for yet another night. As the night drew on, anxious faces would look up towards the abandoned homes fifty yards above and about then, inevitably, someone would bring out a thermos of the universal British panacea; we would all have a nice cup of tea.

One day at dawn, after such a night, we made our way home. Relief! The house was still there. But what was that crowd? Had there been a near miss? Was the house damaged? No. A bomb had landed on the lawn but hadn't exploded. Our hearts were in our mouths and stayed there while someone was called to defuse the monster. We held our breath as he slowly unscrewed a plate on the bomb and reached inside. He had a puzzled expression as he drew a folded slip of paper from a cavity inside.

It carried a message:

"Merci pour ce que vous faites. Continuer comme vous avez commencé".

("Thank you for what you are doing. Carry on as you have begun".)

I have always wondered, my family has always wondered, who the unsung hero was, who sabotaged that bomb. Some brave Frenchman, doubtless a victim of the detested "S.T.O.", the Service de Travail Obligatoire, he risked his life and saved our home. Perhaps more important still, with his message, he helped others to find the courage he had himself, and which we all needed.

The Story of My Cap

Joan Margaret Hicks

As the Germans moved into most of Western Europe in 1940, the original forces that had come over to fight (comprising the British Expeditionary Forces) were suddenly faced with the need to retreat; to get as many of the troops and equipment back to England as possible. This was of course no easy feat; many troops became stranded, holding out as long as possible against the advancing German troops to ensure their comrades made it back. Many felt defeat in their retreating position, although of course there was little alternative. This account highlights the effect this had on retreating troops' morale, and yet the manner in which a soldier and a young civilian could still find some form of comfort from each other, even if for only a brief period of time as their paths crossed in opposite directions.

JUNE 1940

I was 13 years old. The Germans were nearing Paris, French troops were trying to flee to the south of the Loire, the British Army were trying to reach St. Nazaire harbour or other safe harbours to get back to England.

My father, who worked for Cunard Shipping Line, was constantly asking his bosses and the British Embassy in Paris, if he should take his family out of France and to family in England. He was repeatedly told that it was not necessary at that moment and the Embassy would telephone or inform British citizens when to leave Paris.

Days went by and things were not getting any better. After talking with my mother, my father telephoned the Embassy in the rue Faubourg St. Honoré only to find no one was answering. Frustrated by the lack of answers, my father decided to go in person to the Embassy. He hammered on the front door and after what seemed ages a man opened the door a little bit and informed my father that there was no one in the Embassy. They'd all left the previous evening! So much for informing us.

My father came back home to Garche, told my mother to pack what she could, gather us children together and get us ready to leave our home; he went to my grandmother and aunt and informed them to do the same. The family car was prepared and somehow we all climbed in and began our journey to freedom... or so we hoped.

My family, (parents, grandmother and aunt, three brothers and I) were like all of the other civilians, running away from the Nazi invasion. The roads were packed with people trying to get to the ports. Road blocks were inevitable and soon we came to a complete stop.

Suddenly we caught sight of a British military lorry. What excitement for us four children, but how sad, tired out and unshaven these men looked; their eyes were expressionless.

My eyes suddenly crossed to those of a young soldier (he looked about 18; as I say I was 13 but could pass for a "sweet" 16!). A sudden flash between the two of us; the face of this young soldier suddenly lit up with a marvelous smile. I waved to him and he blew me a kiss, which I returned.

We were talking to the soldiers for about an hour when the lorry they were in started to move. Our car also began to move but we were going in the opposite direction. His smile disappeared ... sadness came back into his eyes once more. As I waved him goodbye, he stood up in the back of the lorry, took his Glengarry from his shoulder, kissed it and threw the cap towards me. I caught it by my fingertips. I blew him a farewell kiss.

This happened 73 years ago.

We did not get to St. Nazaire harbour, we were turned back by the Germans and told to go back to our home town.

I have always cherished the cap thrown to me by my young soldier and kept it safe in spite of all we endured during the war. My mother and I were interned but only once I became 16 years of age. We were sent to Vittel and Besançon. Under the Geneva Convention, mothers and children under 16 could not be interned. That of course is another story.

Today, I occasionally have the honour to be Standard Bearer at the Arc de Triomphe in Paris. On the Anniversary of Britain and the Commonwealth entering the First World War (4th August 1914), the Royal British Legion, Paris Branch are invited to rekindle the Flame. I wear this cap with pride.

One day someone said to me: "What a nice cap you have Joan, but it looks rather faded". Perhaps it is, but my eyes do not see it that way. For me it still shines with the marvellous smile of that young soldier.

I am proud to wear this cap and during the silence on the 4th August and 11th November at the Cathedral of Notre Dame in Paris, I give a special thought for my soldier, whoever he was and wherever he may be.

I WILL REMEMBER HIM

Pressing His Suit

Silvana Gillespie

Despite all the misery of the War, the following account details a somewhat more romantic conclusion and outcome to the dark times between 1939-1945. Indeed, if something good did come out of the events of the Second World War, perhaps one such example is the throwing together of two individuals from different backgrounds who would one day end up married and spending the rest of their lives together.

There was nothing romantic about my first meeting with the young man who is now my husband. Our love story started with a pair of trousers and looked like ending with them. I was living in Riccione then, a little town on Italy's Adriatic coast, and the first time I set eyes on Jock was in March 1944, soon after the Allied invasion. He was in the Royal Air Force and, part of our house, having just been left free by two lots of the Royal Electrical and Mechanical Engineers (R.E.M.E.), had then been taken over by the R.A.F.

I never took much notice of the soldiers who were billeted upon us and father didn't wish any of us to mix with them. One day though, a very tall young soldier, fair-haired and good-looking knocked at our kitchen door. He was wearing plimsolls and dressed for a restful afternoon and over one arm he carried a pair of trousers. I had never seen him before and did not know that he was living next door to us.

When I answered his knock, this young man smiled at me shyly and tried to explain in broken Italian what he wanted me to do for him. Actually he had bargained with my father to get his trousers pressed in exchange for a pint of petrol, but I didn't understand this at the time. All I could make out from his funny little speech as he held the pair of trousers forward for me to see was that he wanted me to press them for him. This hurt my young pride. So I shook my head and unceremoniously shut the door upon him.

When I next saw my father he asked me why I had refused to do this small service for the young soldier, with whom he had become quite friendly. Naturally, when I understood the arrangement that had been made, I dutifully pressed the trousers and never had we seen such a long pair.

Jock used to look in rather frequently from then on. Sometimes he would bring me a bar of soap, very precious in those days, and I think that my little sister must have had almost all of his sweet ration. The whole family took to him at once, grandma included. As for me, I thought him "just a nice boy".

On his free nights, he often came to us for supper. In his halting Italian he told me about his girlfriend in England and I told him about a boy I had been fond of, who was in a village still under the Germans' control. We soon decided to try to teach each other our respective languages. We had great fun over this and so did all the family, with whom Jock had now become completely at home. We were luckier than most of our neighbours because, having soldiers occupying some of our rooms, our house had been wired for electricity, though in a very unorthodox fashion. There were no ordinary switches; we had to plug in to get a light. Grandma always went to bed early, leaving us with a sleepy "good night". Jock usually stopped over, chatting with the rest of us until it was time for him to go to his own quarters.

John Gillespie in uniform

Early one morning and without the slightest warning, the Military Police descended upon us. Without saying a word they raced upstairs, searched everywhere, picked up and examined the electric light bulbs, which were fixed into pieces of wood on the bedside tables, and then ordered my father to follow them.

Rather frightened, I asked one of the police what it was all about and all he would say was that I must come along to the police station, too. When we arrived there we learned to our utter consternation and amazement that we were suspected of spying for the Germans! Of course, it was absolutely fantasy and I couldn't imagine why anybody could have thought anything of the sort. Nevertheless, father and I were interrogated separately for two solid hours. The police knew that my father, like almost everybody else at that time, had been a Fascist and they seemed to know many things about our private life, including the fact that I spoke fluent German. At the end of my interrogation, which was conducted, with frequent help from an interpreter, by a bullying sergeant, I was told that, as my father would probably be hanged, I might as well admit that at ten o'clock the previous evening we had been sending signals to the German front line!

John Gillespie, dashing in civvies

That was the last straw. I was really furious and I told the sergeant just what I thought of him and the ridiculous way he was jumping to false conclusions. Not that I wasn't frightened. It seemed hours since they started to question me and when they confronted me with father again, his appearance, tired out, drawn and vacant, tugged at my heartstrings. He had evidently been put through an even harsher questioning than my own.

I *had* to do something at once and it seemed to me that Jock was the only person who could help us. Unfortunately, though, I also knew that British troops were not allowed to spend evenings with civilians. I didn't want to get him into trouble, but what was I to do? As I was frantically trying to think of some other way to prove my father's innocence, a knock came at the door and ... my hero, in his plimsolls again, marched boldly in.

Apparently he had heard from some of his pals that Signor Mordini, my father, had been seen signaling to the Germans about ten o'clock the previous evening; that a sentry had reported this to the Military Police; and that both father and I had been arrested. And Jock had dashed off at once to testify that there couldn't possibly be any truth in this story because he had been with us all evening and nobody, except grandma, had moved from the room until we all went to bed about eleven o'clock. Of course, poor Jock went through the mill with that ferocious sergeant, but my heart was lost to him forever and I could do nothing but gaze up at him adoringly. After some further inquiries had been made, it turned out that grandma had tried with her rather unsteady hands to plug in the light in her bedroom and it was this which had caused the flickering for a few moments. The sentry down the road had thought it was Morse code and reported it.

Jock stayed in Riccione for some weeks longer after all this excitement, but at last the day came when he had to say "goodbye". He looked into my eyes and my heart tore into little pieces. Then he kissed me tenderly just once and left in a hurry. We wrote to each other often while he was away, but he came back to us on his first leave and proposed to me at once. I accepted him wholeheartedly.

Our engagement caused a lot of controversy and roused some opposition. At first his parents and mine were anxious and worried about us and, as for Jock's C.O., the moment he heard that Jock intended to marry an Italian girl, he posted him to Egypt! But my husband is not the sort to be easily daunted and nor am I. We managed to show the lot of them that nothing would make us change our minds.

Gillespie Wedding, 1946

John and Silvana Gillespie, outside Buckingham Palace in 1978, upon Mr. Gillespie's receipt of the O.B.E.

The Freeing of My Parents' Home, "Château de Chantore", by American Forces on 31st July 1944 After the Normandy Landings

Beatrix Keil

How wonderful it must have been on the one hand to suddenly be on the verge of liberation, only to have to plead with such liberators on the other hand to avoid the total destruction of a family's home.

That night we went to sleep in the stable of a nearby farm belonging to my father. The Allied bombardments were fierce. We were protected, in that the German Red Cross had taken over our home and the roofs were covered with red crosses. Allied planes nose-dived overhead ... then went away (we were in the American sector though we didn't know it). That day orders had been given rapidly and the occupying Germans had quickly disappeared. Without protection, and in addition to the fact that the château was very vulnerable on a hill, we risked destruction.

My mother couldn't sleep and got up at five in the morning to go to see what was happening at the château . She came back in an agitated state to tell us that some German soldiers were arriving and it turned out that a straggly column of soldiers was advancing up the avenue. Light cannons were being pulled along by horses, as well as trucks of ammunition and stores. This smacked of defeat ... We later learned that the soldiers had been travelling all night and had come from Brittany.

An officer and a soldier installed themselves in the salon, made a fire in the grate and proceeded to burn papers. In the courtyard a big cauldron was set up and some of the soldiers set to making soup, adding a few of our chickens to the pot. Others, after parking their equipment under the trees and de-harnessing the horses, lay down and slept.

We didn't go back into the château but stayed nearby. It was a beautiful day. My father went across the fields to the village, the roads had for a long time been impracticable and were only used for the movement of troops. He came back with astonishing news: "The Americans are on the main road". This was the main road from Avranches to Granville, 1500 metres from the château.

At last our liberators had arrived! But there were about 100 Germans on our property.

I said to my father, "The Germans here know nothing, they're resting, they're not on the alert. I speak some English. If we go and find the Americans and explain the situation they could capture them by surprise." I was afraid he would refuse, but he accepted. My young sister, my father and I went along the lane leading to the main road which was perpendicular to it. Just before the crossroads an American soldier leapt from the ditch, pointing his gun at us.

I said, in English, "I want to speak to an officer."

A few minutes later a captain came towards me. His unit was probably guarding the crossroads. I didn't know at the time, but these soldiers were part of the Third Army, the celebrated army of General Patton, and the thrust from Avranches is well known in history.

I explained the situation to the captain, not forgetting to mention that the avenue leading to the château was guarded at the point where it joined the lane by two soldiers with a machine gun. A small thing. The other German soldiers were resting unsuspectingly, feeling surely the end was near – but not as near as that! I asked the officer not to fire at the house because only two Germans were there.

He sent my father and young sister back and made me understand I would stay where I was, guarded by a soldier. I was a hostage! I must say this amused me no end. I sat down on the grassy hillock by the side of the road next to my guard. The captain was right; it could have been a trap.

The Americans left for the château, two tanks and an armoured car. I heard a loud cracking sound and was worried about the house. After almost an hour they came back, to my great joy, about a hundred Germans preceding them, their hands on their heads. The American captain was sitting on the roof of his tank and passing near me, he gave me a huge wink – my reward! The Germans were lined up along the road opposite me. They were searched by the captain and another soldier for hidden arms. One German had been wounded and he fainted during the search. Another fascinating spectacle offered itself: motorised American troops passed by going towards Avranches. Splendidly dressed German officers with their capes, their peaked caps placed arrogantly on their heads were sitting on jeep bonnets. What humiliation! The invaders vanquished.

Fascinated by this extraordinary sight, I could have stayed for hours. But I wanted to see what had happened at Chantore. Three tank shells had been fired at the front of the house; one had burst in a room on the ground floor, another had cut the staircase in two and the last one had buried itself, unexploded, in the wall the other side of the staircase. We had to live for several weeks with this unexploded shell before finding an American explosives expert to come and remove it. Practically all the windows at the front of the château were broken. Fortunately the weather was fine and the occupation was at last over for us. I am always moved to tears when I hear this song by Michel Sardou:

> "*Monsieur le Président de France*
> *Je vous écris du Michigan*
> *pour vous dire qu'à côte d'Avranches*
> *Mon père est mort il y a vingt ans*
> *Je n'étais alors qu'un enfant*
> *Mais j'étais fier de raconteur*
> *Qu'il était mort en combattant* ....

Besançon Internment Camp

Joan Margaret Hicks

As we have seen from Joan Hicks' previous account, she endured (with her family) internment from a young age; yet not just in one internment camp, but two. Interestingly Joan Hicks was interned at Besançon, and then released owing to being under the age for such internment, only to be picked up once more by the German army a day after her 16th birthday, as previously warned and in line with the efficiency of German process during the War.

5TH DECEMBER 1940

A date which remains engraved in the memory of many women, children and elderly persons of British nationality, who then lived in France.

British citizens were captured and embarked within half an hour by soldiers of the German Army and French Gendarmerie. We were transported by bus to Maisons-Laffitte, where we were pushed into a train with many other British citizens. We were taken to an internment camp, in the barracks of Besançon in the East of France. The journey had taken two and a half days, arriving at three o'clock in the morning; we had to walk in full darkness from the railway station to the barracks under melting snow and bitterly cold wind. I was only 13 years old, but I remember it very, very clearly.

We remained in these barracks for months until all internees were transferred to another camp in Vittel. Various hotels had been requisitioned by the Germans so as to make a huge internment camp for all British subjects arrested throughout occupied countries of Europe.

After Pearl Harbour, in 1942, American citizens joined us. At the end of the war we were more than 4,000 British and American internees in the Vittel camp.

At Besançon, within a few days, 2,400 British subjects were thrown into that camp; conditions were far from being comfortable, lying on the floor on very thin straw mattresses (not very clean and rather damp). Later we were given bunk-beds. There were very few toilets for some 800 internees per building, so outside latrines were arranged after a few days. Internees had to form long queues in the bitterly cold weather; food was scarce and awful – not to say inedible.

After many months, children under the age of 16, their mothers and elderly persons over the age of 65 were sent back home. We were then informed that when we reached the age of 16, we would be taken back to the camp. This was my case. The German Sergeant came back to our house one day after my 16th birthday. My mother and I were then taken to the Vittel camp where all internees from Besançon had been transferred. The conditions there were much better. We stayed in this camp until Vittel was liberated by General Leclerc's army in September 1944. We were only repatriated to England at the end of October 1944. The welcome we received there was so warm; this is another memory that remains clear in my mind.

In 2005, I visited Besançon and of course I could not resist the urge to visit the barracks. The Colonel in charge of the French Army who was stationed there, invited me to visit the camp which had hardly changed. I was able to go into building B, on the 2nd floor where

I was billeted in 1940 in a huge room which we shared
with 36 other internees (women of all ages, children and
nuns). From our windows (which were half-broken)
we had a good view onto the old Citadel. A beautiful,
but austere historic monument – another sight which I
remember clearly, as I am sure other internees do.

Up till then commemorative plaques had been fixed
in places of other camps, such as Vittel, St. Denis,
Drancy etc; no mention at all in Besançon. Having
raised this point with the Colonel and a representative
of the Besançon municipality, it was suggested that a
plaque recalling these events could be fixed onto one of
the Vauban barracks wall.

On September 8th 2006, the anniversary date of
the liberation of Besançon, a plaque was placed on one
of the walls. The date of the liberation is celebrated
by a ceremony at the Citadel which is a centre for the
memory of those fallen during the war and the local
Resistance. I, of course, appreciate very much this
gesture from the Besançon municipality, as I am sure
that many ex-internees do.

One may wonder: why such an initiative after nearly
70 years?

Within 30 minutes on 5th December 1940, I, like so
many other British subjects living in France, lost *my*
freedom. Our generation is disappearing and I feel, for
the sake of the future generations, that remembrance is
most important. Freedom is a jewel one must protect.
We must be vigilant if we wish to remain free, otherwise
within a few minutes one may find his or herself
deprived of such a "jewel".

A Family Divided By War

Gerald A. Jory

The following account provides a very interesting contrast to the similar accounts featured in this work as regards the internment of British subjects by the Germans. In this case, internment may have been a more bearable option for Mr. Jory and his mother.

My wartime account may be of interest to you, I hope. It is interesting, not so much because of our experiences – some of which were shared, alas, by many others – but because ours is, I believe, a unique case of a London family having been trapped in France and split up for over five years.

We were born and bred in London, but my parents also owned a villa at La Baule in Brittany, to which, we would repair every summer for our holidays. Because of the Munich crisis, it was considered wise not to go abroad in 1938; in the following year however, the crisis seemed to be over, and we made once more for La Baule in late July.

On the eve of the declaration of war, my father returned to London in order to serve in the Royal Army Medical Corps (R.A.M.C.). My two eldest brothers soon also returned, in order to attend their respective schools. There was much talk of London being subjected to air-raids, and it was thought therefore that my mother and we three youngest children (aged 9, 8 and 6) would be safer at La Baule rather than back home where our house was literally in the centre of London (just behind John Lewis in Oxford Street).

The 1940 "Debacle" was for everyone concerned unexpected, violent, chaotic and terrifying. The lack of information and news on what was really happening meant that no-one really knew what the real situation was, nor what to do. On the morning of 15th June, we saw that the British Military Hospital located nearby was being hastily evacuated. My mother rushed over to see the Officer Commanding the Hospital (whom she knew because of my father) and was given a written authority by him to be allowed to board a homeward-bound ship at St. Nazaire. Of the ninety ships or so at anchor, only one of these was embarking civilians: it was the *Lancastria*, a large liner which took on board some 6,000-7,000 men and women – mostly military personnel – but which was bombed and sank with all hands bar some 2,500. We were not on board because we never managed to reach St. Nazaire on time.

On the 5th December, 1940, the French and German police arrested us and locked us up in St. Nazaire and, a few days later, in appalling conditions in Nantes. After a three-day journey locked up in a railway train, we reached Besançon and the Caserne Vauban, which seemed to be a considerable improvement on the ordeal we had just endured. In the following year, we were released, largely through the intervention of the International Red Cross. In a sense, we would have been better off if we had remained interned, for the British subjects – mostly, if not all, of whom had been resident in France – were transferred to Vittel where conditions, we are told, were bearable. In our case, we found ourselves on the Besançon railway platform with a warrant to travel to Paris. We spent the first night in a Red Cross reception centre in one of the waiting rooms of the Gare de Lyon, and we eventually found some French friends of our parents who very generously took the four of us in to share their flat, until we could sort ourselves out. Life was complicated by the fact that my mother had no source of income; re-establishing contact with my father was difficult, if not well nigh impossible. Money had somehow to be borrowed. We were required initially to report daily to the local Commissariat, and my mother was forbidden to work; the work she occasionally managed to obtain was unauthorized and therefore undeclared.

The worst ordeal however was the scarcity of news from England. At one time, we spent some two years without news at all from my father and elder brothers. My father served with the 8th Army in North Africa and Italy and then took command of General Hospitals in the Lebanon and in Egypt. Joyce Grenfell, who at some stage toured the Middle East, referred to him in her autobiography!

The years 1943 and 1944, when I was 13 and 14, provided moments of particular excitement for me, because I acted as an interpreter for a Resistance network in the Loiret providing an escape route for allied airmen whose planes had been shot down.

Shortly after the Liberation of Paris, we were flown back to Croydon in a R.A.F. Dakota, and the family was reunited in 1945; the only note of bitterness I have in this account concerns the refusal of the military authorities to grant my father compassionate leave when we returned: we did not see him until he was demobilised in the following year.

As you may imagine, I treasure the various documents which I hold and which bear out what I believe to be an unusual war-time experience.

France to England via Spain – Three Refugees

John C. Clark

Mr. Clark's account provides a very profound insight into life on the run from the occupying German forces, the collusion and collaboration on the part of Marechal Petain, French patriotic resistance (if only through forms of measured demonstration), the arduous task of getting from France across the border to neutral (though Fascist) Spain, and ultimately the safe passage to Great Britain.

GOOD NEWS: THE CHARACTERS

"This is the B.B.C. Home and Forces programme, and this is Bruce Belfrage: there is some excellent news just in from Cairo. After twelve days of bitter fighting, the enemy is in complete retreat before the Eighth Army."

This was how I learned of the victory of El Alamein, one evening at the beginning of November 1942 at 11 o'clock. My father maintains that it was midnight because there was no scheduled news broadcast at eleven but, as this was a special bulletin, and anyway my father had been in the "land of nod" for at least an hour and half, I still believe I was right.

We were in France at the time; in Lyon to be precise.

My parents and I had always lived in France, near Paris, until June 1940. My father was English, my mother French. They both, in normal times, worked in insurance. We had left Paris, our home and our friends in June 1940 just before the arrival of the Germans and we found asylum, firstly with friends, at the Château de la Gardelle, and later in a small village on the fringe of Périgord at Alvignac-les-eaux. It was a pleasant little village in the Causses and not very far from that better known and highly picturesque village, Rocamadour. The latter is entirely built on a cliff face and its castle, at the highest point, dominates a gray mixture of belfries, churches, the roofs of convents and a few houses.

Near Alvignac is the famous Puits de Padirac, which is a giant sinkhole in the limestone, more than three hundred metres deep. It can be visited, and most people get to the bottom by means of the lift, which has been installed. At the bottom there is a river, which can be followed for five kilometres deep underground. You can even take a boat up this river and a good part of the network of caves has been equipped with railings and electric lighting. In Alvignac, we took refuge in a hotel which could take up to 45 guests in the summer. When we arrived there were a hundred and fifty. In spite of the circumstances, we enjoyed our stay and I particularly remember some wonderful bicycle rides to the well-known caverns nearby, such as Lacaze and Les Eyzies. Many others which we explored had not yet entered the tourist itinerary.

After two months in Alvignac, after the Armistice and with the permission of the local gendarmerie, we were given petrol coupons and permission to proceed to Lyon. Lyon had just been evacuated by the "Boches" and was on the way to becoming the capital of the non-occupied zone as we called it at the time (once the situation had become clear we called it "the not completely occupied zone"). The city was overrun with refugees of all kinds. After spending some time in the villa of a friend of ours, we managed to find an apartment close to the Rhône where we were relatively comfortably installed.

Until the beginning of November 1942, life in Lyon was more or less normal, apart from the restrictions because we were English. Registered voters and known to the Prefecture of Police, we had never been bothered by officials.

On the other hand, everyone we knew used to ask us about the intentions of His Britannic Majesty's Government which, they seemed to imagine, kept us informed of its deliberations. Many of these contacts were very useful because they enabled us to keep in touch with the Resistance and to read all the clandestine newspapers such as *Combat, Franc-Tireur, Libération,* and *Libre France.* Thanks to the regular news broadcast by the BBC, we were always able to be optimistic. This was not the case with the French public in general. Saturated as it was with Vichy anti-English propaganda, public opinion went from one extreme to the other.

Prominent in the German Propaganda version of the news were events such as the bombardment of the French Fleet at Mers el Kébir, Crete, the taking of Hong Kong and Singapore. Tobruk did nothing to reassure the French. In my opinion one of the greatest German victories when it came to destroying French morale was the passage of the boats *Scharnhorst, Gneisnau* and *Prinz Eugen* into the English Channel, within spitting distance of the English ports. "Ah", someone said, "The English Navy must have completely lost control of the seas since the German Navy can come and go as it likes in the English Channel".

But if these reverses were precursors of a wave of pessimism, the other side of the coin was represented by events such as the sinking of the *Bismark,* and these compensated more than a little for the bad news. My father always remembers a large truck driving down the rue de la République in Lyon with the magic word "Spitfire" written in chalk on the roof.

And so things continued until that beautiful morning of Sunday November 8th, 1942. In spite of the combined efforts of Vichy and the Germans to scramble all the wireless programs, everyone quickly heard the news of the disembarking of the Allied troops in North Africa, followed by General Giraud's appeal to the French nation. That morning, after mass, everyone wore bright and happy smiles, all were anxious to pass on the good news to those rare souls who had not yet been informed. Variants on the theme, "You've heard the news? Not bad, eh?", were everywhere. Yes, it was even going very well, after all the reverses we had suffered. I remember a student friend saying to me in June 1942, while the Germans were advancing on Egypt: "It's a matter of days, maybe even hours till they take Cairo, Alexandria and the Suez Canal". I never spoke to him again. Good news indeed, but for my family, it meant that complications were likely to ensue. The next day I went off to work as usual and, apart from the fact that tongues were wagging incessantly, things were rather calm. It was only on Tuesday that our adventure started, an adventure which was, in the end to get us back to good old England.

MARSHAL PÉTAIN

At this point, I would like to make a few observations on Marshal Pétain.

Pétain had considerable authority and many supporters in Lyon. He had a great reputation and was venerated because of the part he played in the 1914-18 war. He had also picked a moment, when nobody had the slightest idea what to do, to declare his *coup d'état* and to ask for an armistice. It should not be forgotten that he had been severely reprimanded by Poincaré for defeatism and that, when Clémençeau had to choose an overall Commander in 1918, he said : "Before me were two men : one wanting an armistice (Pétain), the other driven mad by the very idea (Foch); I chose the mad one and we won the war".

It was he, Pétain, who before the war severely criticised the books of General de Gaulle on the future of tank warfare.

It was he who shook the Fuhrer's hand at Montoire.

It was he who said, "We must help the Germans who are fighting for civilisation".

It was he who said, "Every morning, I tell myself that we were beaten."

It was he who re-engaged Laval, after having dismissed him because he was not serving the interests of France.

Misusing his prestige as "First Marshal of France" it was he, above all others, responsible for the defeat which France had undergone.

PRELIMINARY ADVENTURES

On Tuesday morning, I went to work as usual, but there was a kind of indefinable atmosphere, a funny sort of feeling which I could not escape, and at midday, instead of going back home for lunch, I dropped in at my father's office, where he informed me that we were leaving for Grenoble that afternoon. We had chosen Grenoble because rumours had it that the Germans would only occupy the Rhône-Saône valley and the Riviera. In addition, we had excellent friends there.

In Lyon that day, there were groups of French soldiers wandering the streets with nothing to do and nowhere to go, penniless and, worse, without ration books. They couldn't even go into restaurants, as they were all asking for ration coupons. The German soldiers had invaded their barracks that morning and given them five minutes to leave; if they had not gone by then the Germans evicted them, throwing their possessions out of the windows. It would have been the perfect moment for a revolution, in my opinion – although I must admit I am somewhat lacking in practical experience of revolutions.

And yet, I cannot continue without mentioning the demonstrations which I did see. This rather contradicts the foregoing as a demonstration is, in fact, a sort of miniature revolution, and if a demonstration is well planned, it can become a thoroughgoing revolution. Look at South America.

In any case, during the four years of occupation, the French took advantage of every chance to express themselves: May 1st, July 14th and November 11th were their favourite dates. These were not enough for the French and they dug into their memories and their history books to find favourable dates; a victory over the Germans in the 1700s; the anniversary of some Marshal who had fought the Germans; anything would do. They could have done with one of my history teachers, a man who would have found them an event for every day of the year.

The biggest demonstration which I remember happened on July 14th, 1942. My mother was at Perrache station and I was at the Place de la République. I saw them arrive at the Place Bellecour, completely filling the Rue de la République. Red, white and blue flags floating over their heads, they were singing the Marseillaise. When they reached the Place de la République, hundreds of Gendarmes and Police appeared from nowhere and started to disperse them, carrying off dozens in their police vans. They dispersed into the side-streets to regroup later. The police force did a lot of overtime that day to keep things under control. Another great demonstration had been scheduled for November 11th, but the sudden occupation of the so called "free-zone" by the Germans and the Italians interfered with this and, this time, in most towns the demonstrations never saw the light of day.

We arrived at Grenoble the same evening in a train, which was more than crowded (as they all were then), and found two rooms in the hotel, which was to become the Italian Headquarters. While we were there, we saw quite a lot of Italians. The French have never liked the Italians and never will. I always remember the banner that the French had hung on the French-Italian frontier when the Greeks resisted the Italian invasion and pushed them back: "Greeks! Stop here. This is France", said the banner.

We had the privilege of seeing the victorious Italian army parading in the streets of Grenoble, laughing and singing, traditional feather in hat. More on this subject later. After one week in Grenoble, seeing that nothing was happening, we returned to Lyons. The people of Lyon, who had not been very active until then started to show signs of life. This was sometimes violent; almost every night a bomb would explode: at the recruitment office for voluntary work in Germany, the office of a newspaper which had sold out to the Germans, a kiosk where German newspapers were sold, the headquarters of the Parti Populaire Français, and even in a butcher's shop reputed to sell to the Germans on the black market. One evening, we heard a bigger than usual explosion. Later we learned that it was one of the arsenals that had been blown up. News of this never reached the newspapers.

One could read odd things in the papers then; Rommel was retreating across Cyrenaica and Libya. For fifteen days, the official news repeated with little variation: "Marshal Rommel has successfully carried out his tactic of disengagement." "The English have failed to engage his rear guard." Then, after a pause, at El Agheila: "Marshal Rommel leads the battle towards Tripoli." And finally the juiciest of them all: "Marshal Rommel continues his advance westwards." I really must insist: this is not a tall story, it really appeared like that in the pro-German press in Lyon.

By now the Germans and the Italians had occupied all of France except Toulon, which remained the only place in France, or indeed the French Empire, still controlled entirely and only by France. All the colonies were occupied by the English, the Americans, the Germans, the Italians or the Japanese.

This is the moment that Laval called upon French workers to go to work in Germany, an appeal which went under the motto: "I want German victory". Understandably of limited popularity, few Frenchmen of the time will have forgotten this.

Of course there was the other side of the story at the other side of the Channel, where there was a young Colonel promoted to Général right at the beginning of the war. If he was still almost unknown in France, he had already earned the respect of the Germans: General Charles de Gaulle. Many French people turned to him in June to July of 1940, seeing him as a saviour. It was he who answered Marshal Pétain's, "Not enough weapons, not enough planes, not enough allies", with the words: "France has lost a battle, but it has not lost the war. Join me, I will continue the combat beside the entire British Empire until France is liberated". These were the words France was waiting for. De Gaulle continued the combat. He would not let go before the obvious superiority of the enemy; he was the man of the moment. France needed a man like him, full of energy; it got Pétain however.

There were a good number of partisans in France, even at the beginning and, in 1942, they were organised and armed. They included the President of the Chambre de Députés, Mr. Edouard Herriot and the President of the Senate, Mr. J. Jeanneney. Both had sent a letter to the Marshal Pétain explaining why what he was doing was illegal and that, in a country like France, he could not simply appoint himself "Head of State" without the assent of the People. The majority of the men and women who were to form the Resistance and later the Forces Françaises de l'Intérieur (F.F.I.) came from the working classes. They had lived in freedom since 1918 and they saw this freedom was unlikely to survive the arrival of the Germans. Students, who formed a specific group within society, were somewhat divided but those who were really for General de Gaulle did a great deal for the morale of France. The peasant population at the time was still substantial. It is to be regretted that many of them benefited from the occupation to enrich themselves, through black market operations with the Germans, which left their countrymen more needy than they might otherwise have been.

On November 18th, 1942, my father and I visited a prison camp where 250 English soldiers and four Russians were interned. I never have quite understood how the latter had arrived there as, at the time, the Russian front was several thousand kilometres away. After we had obtained from the French military authorities, the necessary permit to visit the camp, and a second authorization to go there by car (the latter being something of a feat in itself), we arrived at the camp on a cold morning in November to learn that we would not be allowed to visit the camp after all but simply be allowed to speak to the senior English officer about the internees.

We had learned that the camp was very badly run but, as it was only an internment camp (France being more or less neutral in principle), conditions should have been a little better than in a prison camp. In fact, the poor conditions prevailing in the camp were mainly due to its being moved from its location near Nice to a new site near Grenoble (a move motivated by the massive escape of fifty internees, of whom only ten were subsequently recaptured). The officer in charge was a Captain of the Royal Navy; once we had been introduced, we were taken to an over-heated room where we were to converse. We were six in all: the English officer, a French officer, my father, me, a guard and the official interpreter. He was a fellow of about fifty, English by birth but naturalised French and who lived in Calais.

After half an hour's conversation, the English officer seemed to lose interest and kept his eyes on the French officer who, according to him, was a real brute. Conversation languished. My father had taken note of all his complaints, and silences in the conversation became increasingly long and oppressive until the interpreter, who had said nothing so far, suddenly announced, "You can say what you like, you know. The two others don't understand a word of English and I don't mind what you say". Thereupon the English officer forgot all about the French officer and the interview lasted for another hour. The last time I heard of this officer, he was a parliamentary candidate in England. He had escaped with seven others. After this visit, we moved about quite a bit to ensure that the occupying forces didn't take too much interest in our presence. Every time we left Lyon on some project to leave France, it was with the heartfelt good wishes of our friends, and at each return it was to explain our failure to get away and our plans to try something else next week.

From time to time, we got interesting offers to get us to Switzerland, but one could not leave there and what we really wanted was to get back to Britain. The fastest means was obviously by air, but the plan that we had once made to do this had failed because of the weather. Then there was the sea, but this also failed, as will be explained in the next chapter.

Finally, my father left for Agen to see whether there wasn't some means of getting to Spain. He came up with something and sent a message which resulted in my mother and I taking the train from Lyon to Perigord on 2nd December 1942 at 6.18 pm. We had tried the plane, the boat and the train already; this time it was to be on foot.

THE SUN, A BOAT, THE MOON AND COMMANDOS

Before writing about our final departure from Lyon, I should mention that we were involved in another earlier adventure.

It started in July 1942, when my father and I were on a cycling holiday in the centre of France. While my mother was alone at the office, a young man came in and announced that he would like to meet us as he was English. Given the activity of the Gestapo at the time, this was not a very reassuring statement and the last thing likely to induce confidence in my mother's mind. She sent him away but said he could drop by again when my father was there. Contrary to expectations, this is just what he did and, after several visits, he finally persuaded us of his good faith. He was a spy and had been parachuted into France. From then on, we helped him with his wireless transmissions to England.

He often spoke about getting us out and to England and, after November 1942, the situation having become more urgent, we asked him how he thought this might be done. By submarine, he said, and although my mother was less than enthusiastic at this, it was a better solution than to let ourselves be imprisoned. Thus it was on 2nd November, that André, our young English officer, invited us to spend a few days with him in Nice. We left that very day carrying with us two of his wireless transmission sets. The trip went very well: we even managed to get seats on the train by the simple expedient of arriving at the station an hour early. We were not, however, very comfortable, given that we were travelling with false identity cards and had two wireless sets in our bags, especially since the train went through Toulon where the French fleet had just been scuttled.

At the beginning, we tried to sleep but it was too hot. We tried to get some fresh air in the corridor only to find that it was just as hot there and that the corridors were just as crowded as the compartments. We tried to open the windows but this was prohibited because the trains did not have curtains. The window glass was painted blue for the blackout which at least provided a unique opportunity to express one's political opinions by scraping them in the paint. The only significant event of the trip was at Toulon where the train stopped. Would the Germans check our papers? Always a bit worrying when they are forged. Would they search the passengers' luggage? Not very reassuring either given that you have your English passports there, not to mention a couple of radio transmitters. Despite our fears, all went well and the train stopped in Toulon only for the scheduled time.

It was an unfamiliar Toulon compared with that which I had known before the war. A huge black cloud emanated from the docks and the arsenal, obscuring the city and its suburbs. Then there were German sailors on the station platforms in their black uniforms and caps with the word "Kriegsmarine" on them in gold. They were somewhat lost as they no longer had a boat to go to. We arrived at Nice only two hours late. Ah, Nice! The Mediterranean, sun, flowers; a real paradise.

What a difference from the dark and narrow streets of Lyon, the surly Saône and muddy Rhône; rain, cold, snow and fog. Here, broad avenues bordered with flowers, the blue of the sea and a gentle warmth even at the beginning of December.

The only black spot was the Italian occupation: Italian soldiers, two to a motorcycle roaring at full speed along the Promenade des Anglais or strolling "on patrol" along the shore, cigarette hanging from their lips. Smiling at the girls and on the whole looking very pleased with themselves. We learned later that they weren't as happy as all that; it seems their food left a lot to be desired.

We spent two days basking in the sun. Then, as we were having lunch on the Promenade des Anglais, André turned up to announce that everything was ready for our departure. We left Nice on a Monday and went to an *auberge*, the "Moulin à Cros" at Cagnes sur Mere, six or seven kilometres along the coastal road. It was there that we met those who were to be our travelling companions: two French police inspectors who had allowed fifteen English agents to escape and who consequently risked having serious problems with their wives (that is, they were accompanied by their wives, not that their wives necessarily objected to their political conduct); and a French officer and two young Frenchmen who had been parachuted in from England. All in all there were ten of us.

The *auberge* was pleasant and the owners welcoming. They lit a fire in a huge fireplace and served us a good meal to send us off. In fact it had everything one could hope for in a first class holiday hotel and it was with some little reluctance that, at 11 o'clock in the evening, we abandoned our refuge and headed for the beach. We left in three groups; I was in the last to leave. We went down a narrow and difficult path with many a slip and fall but finally reached a fisherman's cottage, which was our rendezvous, to find that one of the other groups had not yet arrived. Somehow we had passed them on the way. It was a worrying moment but they eventually appeared in good order and we settled down to wait.

The arrangement was to be as follows: we were to remain in the fisherman's cottage while, from another location, André and one of his comrades made signals seawards, until a boat from the submarine landed. For some reason, however, this didn't work and it was decided that we should leave in the fisherman's boat and go to meet the submarine, taking advantage of information that the Italian patrol boat was occupied elsewhere.

We must have been a strange sight that midnight. There were fifteen of us now, including three women, carrying the fisherman's cobble on our shoulders across the road and down some steps to the sea, in constant fear of being spotted by a foot patrol. Finally, all those due to leave got in the boat. I might add that it was a very ordinary boat, built to take five people. We were eleven. The boat was leaking too and the sea was rough enough to make several of our passengers sick. The conversation during the next two or three hours would have been worthy of a book, which would necessarily be titled: "Seven men and three women in a boat" (excluding the fisherman). The first hour was not too bad; the fisherman rowed seawards in search of the submarine or its boat. André's signals from the shore were clearly visible. We had a nasty moment when a light suddenly appeared. Our first thought was that it was an Italian high-speed motorboat looking for us but the light faded away and our optimism returned.

This went on until one thirty in the morning, at which time the moon rose slowly over the sea. Beautiful, you might think, the moon rising over the Mediterranean on a balmy night. To our jaundiced eye it carried another message: silhouetted against the moonlit sky we were far too visible from the shore. Then the signals from André's position on the shore stopped abruptly. For an hour and half, we rowed hither and thither in search of the phantom submarine. (Much later we learned that it had actually been there but that it had not seen any of our signals). And if we returned to the beach, in the absence of the reassuring signals from the shore party we didn't know what was waiting for us. Would we find an Italian patrol? Had our friends been arrested and were the Italians quietly waiting for us? In the end, we had little option and we headed back. Our faithful fisherman brought us to the exact spot on the beach that we had left from.

It was something of a commando landing. As soon as the boat grounded those in front leapt out and dragged it onto the sand. Everyone disembarked in record time and ran for shelter behind a low wall which ran along the road. Sure enough, as we got our bearings, an Italian patrol came along and we all held our breath as it passed safely by, unaware of our presence. Then the shore party appeared, safe and sound. We pulled the boat further up the beach and once again took refuge in the fisherman's cottage.

There, we were given a much-needed hot cup of coffee and there we spent the remainder of the night, soaked and stiff from our ill-fated trip round the bay.

Our friends who had remained on shore could not understand why we had lost sight of the signals because they had sent them continuously. Upon reflection it would seem that we had drifted out of the angle which they covered. London was contacted by wireless and we were told there was a chance we might be picked up four days later. On the appointed night we spent another night in the cottage but nothing came of this.

Disappointed, we spent another two days in Nice before returning to Lyon to the great astonishment of all our friends to whom we had said good-bye.

As I mentioned earlier, my mother and I left to join my father at Agen on the 2nd December 1942 by the 6.18 pm train for Périgueux. The time is of some importance, as will be seen. Most unusually for the period, we had a compartment to ourselves. At one of the stops on the way, Montlucon, we were delighted to find relatives who had made a special trip to the station at one o'clock in the morning to bring us cakes and hot coffee.

Then we had to change for Limoges where the train stood two hours in the dark and frozen station. I have been to Limoges twice in my life. The first time was on June 14th, 1940 when we stopped there to have breakfast, the second time was this one; two hours in the freezing station.

We arrived at Agen at about two o'clock in the afternoon and stayed there for Christmas with some friends. I remember their son bloodthirstily referring to the Germans as 'apprentice corpses'. These friends had a grocer's shop. One day they asked a newly arrived young German soldier how old he was. He laughed and answered: "I am 14 years old for my mother, 15 for my Fuhrer, but I am still old enough to kill a Frenchman".

Christmas Day fell on a Friday. It was the following Sunday that we left Agen for Pau. There was a change of trains at Toulouse, which left us enough time to go to the cinema where we saw "*La Kermesse Héroïque*" (The Heroic Village Fair).

The next morning, we met the organiser of our passage into Spain. He started by telling us to get rid of our hats. When we asked what we should do with our luggage, which by then had been reduced to a single leather case, a briefcase and a rucksack, he said that was fine: it was a simple matter of a six-hour walk along a footpath and that, in any event we could get mules to carry our things. Once we got to Spain, a taxi would be waiting to take us directly to the British Consulate in Pamplona.

From there we left for Oloron-Sainte-Marie, where we lunched and then to Mauleon, where we stayed until nine o'clock in the evening, in a hotel where we knew nobody. At last a car came to take us to a Basque farm in the little village of Ossa. Sitting around the fire we listened to the conversation of two guides and the farmer's wife. We understood nothing of it for they spoke in Basque. One of them was able to make himself understood in French and it was to him that we suggested borrowing mules to carry our luggage, as we had been led to understand this was possible. When he translated our request there was a general shout of laughter.

Mule-less, then, we set off on our crossing of the Pyrenees at one o'clock in the morning. My mother was wearing warm clothes, light shoes, silk stockings and a fur coat. My father wore what he would usually wear to go to the office in winter. I had a raincoat attached to my rucksack and was wearing a normal overcoat.

Our guides had said that our first objective was a shepherd's hut where they kept their sheep in summer. It was, they indicated, about two hours walk. The first obstacle was the mud. For two hours, we made our way up the mountain, on what was undoubtedly a path in summer but which was now alternately a torrent and a bog. As we got higher, we started to see ice. Soon every square centimetre of solid ground or rock was covered with a fine layer of black ice and for another two hours still we continued, slipping back one pace for every two made upwards. Worried at the failure of the promised cabin to materialise, we asked what was happening. Our guide admitted that he was lost. There was no alternative, however, but to press on and finally, by some miracle, we arrived at the hut after six and a half hours of climbing. We lit a small fire and had something to eat.

We set out again at eight o'clock and continued to walk in frozen rain until half past twelve. We arrived at a second hut, where we made a fire again and ate.

We had two guides with us: Gaston, twenty years old, who was supposed to be our official guide, and Baptiste, who was about forty. Baptiste had an extraordinary way of lighting a fire. He took a few pieces of dry wood or, if he couldn't find any, broke up one or two panels from the walls and started a tiny fire. Then he would bring in some huge wet log from outside and dump it on the little blaze. For anybody else it would have immediately killed the fire. For Baptiste, and against all likelihood, it invariably burst into flame. It was all the more remarkable as there were no fireplaces in the huts.

The afternoon programme consisted of climbing the Pic des Escaliers. We left at two o'clock and the climb lasted until five thirty. The morning rain had become hail and a violent wind blew from our right. The melting hail soaked our clothes – even, in my case, through my raincoat and overcoat combined. We learned why the Pic des Escaliers, "Staircase Peak" was thus named. It reached a turning and we could see as much in front as we could behind. This exhausting series of zig-zags lasted three hours and half.

Despite everything, we finally arrived at the top and there the guides informed us that the frontier was not very far. We were all tired, however, even the guides, so we decided to stop at the next hut, which we reached at six-thirty accompanied by swirling blasts of snow, which had started to fall as soon as we passed the summit. We decided to stay in this hut for the night. Baptiste did his trick with the fire and we soon had a splendid blaze, which almost set the ceiling alight. Later that evening, we had a nasty shock when we heard voices from outside. Then we heard sheep baaing and were able to relax. They were only shepherds smuggling sheep. They joined us in the cabin and spent the night there with us. We tried hard to sleep, but it wasn't easy as we were beginning to wonder how this "two hour walk" was going to end. It was, after all some 24 hours now since we had set off and we still hadn't reached the frontier.

It was while we were in this hut that Gaston announced that he was "a bit tired" so he would let us continue without him, but with the two shepherds and Baptiste. As our supplies were running low, we decided to leave a little earlier and we set out again at three thirty. The first three hours were rather pleasant. The snow had stopped and the landscape was beautiful; wild mountains covered with snow, black pines clinging to their slopes contrasting with the white, the whole crowned with a cloudless sky filled with stars. We could have admired it for hours. We didn't.

Trouble came with the dawn. Snow had started to fall again. We had to cross a river four or five times and then pass the German customs station in silence and without being seen. Afterwards there was another mountain to climb in a forest and the sheep (there were 11 of them and they had probably had nothing to eat for days) refused to advance. We each took a stick and climbed this mountain having to lift our feet high out of the knee-deep snow while at the same time poking and beating the sheep in front of us. Somehow we reached the plateau in a snow storm, which restricted visibility to four or five metres.

Our situation had become critical. Finally, after a short conference, the shepherds decided to abandon their sheep and to continue without them. For two hours we walked and several times realised that we had gone in a circle, without ever getting back to our starting point.

My mother announced that she could go no further and asked us to leave her there in the snow. Baptiste had frostbitten hands and said we were all finished. The shepherds wanted to walk as straight and as fast as possible until nightfall. My father helped my mother to advance; I prayed God to get us out of this dreadful situation and did my best to maintain a contact between the shepherds and Baptiste on the one hand, and my mother and father who were lagging further and further behind on the other.

The miracle happened at half past eleven. The snowstorm had redoubled in violence and we had lost contact with the group in front. Suddenly the eddies of snow parted to reveal a patch of perfectly blue sky which illuminated part of the plateau and a valley at the bottom of which there was a hut. Baptiste and the shepherds immediately headed towards it. We followed as well as we could, for the slope was steep and it was as much by slipping and sliding that we finally arrived at the hut, just as the snowstorm resumed, more violent than ever.

After a rest of an hour and a half, when the storm had calmed a little, we set out again and at quarter past four on Wednesday December 30th, 1942, we crossed the Spanish border. It was with a sigh of relief for we thought our troubles were over. We had no idea what was waiting for us.

At about seven o'clock we reached the first Spanish house where we were able to get a hot meal. The room was lit only by pine twigs burning on a metal sheet and it was cold, but we were able to savour the pleasure of sleeping with sheets and blankets for the first time since we had woken the previous Monday morning.

The first Spanish house was located on a reservoir and it was by boat that we set out again at about midday the following day. We left Baptiste and the shepherds there and went with the daughter of the house, who would do nothing but smile for no apparent reason. She rowed us to the house of the guardian of the reservoir dam where we had been told there was a telephone, which we would be able to use to phone the British Consulate in Pamplona or to get a taxi to take us there directly. That is what we believed. It's not the way it happened.

At the guardian's house we were given a meal of eggs and bacon (an English speciality we had hardly expected to find on the Franco-Spanish border). We would have to, we were told, walk to the next village because the car had not yet been constructed capable of getting to the dam, even in summer, not to mention winter.

For some time now, we were becoming a little bitter, a sentiment concerning the world in general and the Basques in particular. My mother was rather tired so we decided to rent a mule on which my mother could ride. To this day she swears she would have done better to go on foot. We were accompanied this time by a charming gentleman, a businessman to judge by appearances. He talked incessantly during the entire trip, a conversation which was somewhat lost on us as neither my father, my mother nor myself spoke a word of Spanish, a fact which did not discourage him at all.

We were approaching the village when we saw two "carabineros" (frontier police) coming to meet us. Without a word (which would, admittedly, have been useless) they fell in beside us. They were dressed in long (too long), green overcoats, rifle on shoulder, cigarette in mouth and each carried an enormous blue umbrella – a surreal addition to their armament. As further security, one of them even had a walking stick.

Arriving at the first town, Orbaicetta (we had left the Pentano dam), it was with great difficulty that we were given to understand that we could not remain there; we would have to go to the regional headquarters some thirty kilometres further on. It subsequently became clear that what they really wanted was for us to pay for a car to cover the distance and five or six people took advantage of the opportunity to accompany us.

The officer in charge of the region was charming and after having us empty all our pockets (or almost), he showed us to a room which we had been allocated at a farm in the village.

The following day being January 1st, everything in Spain came to a halt and we had to spend the New Year at this farm, where the only person who could understand us, and whom we could understand, was a deaf and dumb man. That morning, however, we learned that four Americans had arrived in the night. We immediately went to see them to find that they were no more American than we were. There was an Austrian Jew, two Luxembourg brothers and a Frenchman.

On January 2nd, we were taken from Villanueva to Valcarlos, a village dominating the valley, which formed the frontier at this point and from where we could see the German guards. For a few bad moments we wondered if it was not the intention of our hosts to send us back.

Sunday being another day on which everything stops in Spain, we had to wait until January 4th to be escorted to Pamplona. Our group having grown day by day, were now sixteen, including three women and we all arrived in the evening at the Commissaria de Vigilancia (the police station). There, we were all informed that the hotels of Pamplona were full to overflowing and that there was only one solution to accommodate us until our departure for Madrid the next morning. That was the prison.

The following is largely a transcription of notes taken during our imprisonment on toilet paper, since the authorities did not allow writing paper.

1) A stroll around cell 64.

This was the cell we had been attributed eleven days before, on Monday January 4th 1943, at eleven o'clock in the evening.

Right from the beginning of this trip, we had been told nothing but lies: lies when the organiser had told us that we could go directly to the British Consulate in Pamplona. No such consulate has ever existed; Lies when he told us that it was only a six hour walk in the Pyrenees. Still more lies since we got to Spain. Everyone knew perfectly well what was going to happen to us, from the first farmer who sold us, the businessman who accompanied us, the two 'carabinieri' who took us in charge and even the police chief of Pamplona, who had the gall to tell us, with excuses, that we would have to spend a night in prison because all the hotels were full.

On leaving the police station, we were escorted to the prison. We went through five or six barred doors and had to leave my mother at the entrance to the women's section. We were searched (not very thoroughly) and put in a cell where we were to sleep, six of us with one straw mattress and ten blankets.

The cell was on a wide corridor forming the vertical bar of a 'T', which was three stories high and guarded from a central office. Above this was an altar. The door of cell 64, ours, was made of wood and was 12 centimetres thick. A small opening at chest height allowed the guards to pass us our food. The walls were of solid stone and 75 centimetres thick. The cell ran from

94

East to West, the door being at the western end. It was about 5 metres long, 2.5 metres wide and 3.5 metres high. On the ceiling was a single small lamp and there was a window, 75x50 cm, on the eastern wall. On the southern wall was a wooden bed which folded against this wall and in the north-western corner, the W.C., if it could be called that. Above the door was a small shelf on which all our luggage had to be stored. Lastly, on the northern side, was a table fixed to the wall. The remaining furniture consisted of a stool, a bucket and a brush.

On arrival, six of us were allocated to this cell despite our noisy objections. As we settled down, as well as we could, we comforted ourselves with the thought that at least we were in Spain and, after all, we were to leave the next day.

2) Prison life.

The next morning a trumpet sounded reveille at 7 am. At five past we were ready to leave. At seven thirty we were handed six metal bowls of tepid and dirty water. Was it to wash? Shave? Perhaps to wash the floor? Sometime later, we were given six spoons and we realised that it was breakfast, but by then we had thrown the contents of the bowls down the hole in the corner which served as a toilet.

Around nine o'clock we found ourselves on parade with other new arrivals at the prison in front of the office where, while we awaited our turn, we struck up a conversation with a prisoner who, with that smile that only one prisoner can have for another, told us that he had no idea how long we were likely to stay there but that it could be anything from fifteen days to three months. We couldn't believe that and, when we were returned to our cell, after having answered a few questions, we hopefully held ourselves ready to leave at a moment's notice.

Our hopes were somewhat dashed when the prison barber entered our cell, escorted by a guard with a sinister smile, which would have prohibited him from making his living as anything other than a prison guard. The barber successively treated us all to a 'zero' cut, which left less than a centimetre of hair: It was a horrible sensation and a nasty sight, the only consolation being that a comb was now entirely superfluous.

The prison routine:

06h 50	Lights on
07h 00	Reveille is sounded on a trumpet
07h 15	1st inspection
07h 30	Breakfast (see above)
08h 00	A bucket of water arrives
09h 00	2nd inspection
10h 00	3rd inspection and patio until midday
12h 30	Lunch (boiled potatoes and broad beans)
14h 30	Water (see 08h00)
15h 00	4th inspection and patio till 18h00
18h 15	Distribution of bread (200 grams each)
18h 45	Dinner (boiled potatoes without beans)
20h 25	National Anthem
20h 30	Last inspection
21h 00	Lights out

Sunday's routine differed from the other days by the fact that we had to get up half an hour earlier; this was for mass at 8 am. At 9 am the prison orchestra replaced the priest on the altar and gave a concert. Lunch on Sunday consisted of boiled potatoes and ordinary (not broad) beans.

The 'Patio' mentioned above consisted of a small courtyard. We were allowed to walk there during the above specified times. Clandestine border-crossers like ourselves were grouped together for this walk. There were 450 unshaven men (except Wednesdays, the day we got to shave) walking around trying to keep warm in this patio. They were of all nationalities although they all claimed to be Canadian or American. Besides my father and myself, there was only one other person of English nationality in the prison. What amused us was that whether you were Hindu or Buddhist, Moslem or Protestant, you were obliged to attend the Catholic mass. The service lasted one hour and the subsequent concert another, during which we were still standing in the corridors in ranks of ten it was the prisoners turn to sing: first the national anthem, then the fascist anthem, during which we were supposed to raise our arms in salute.

Return to cells was in single file, accompanied by a march, by Souza. Then the guards closed the cell doors, making sure that everyone was within and crying 'todos' (all there).

3) A prisoner's diary, written at the Pamplona Provincial Prison Friday 22nd January, 1943

It was odd how the minutiae of everyday events took on an importance out of all proportion. Here is mine for 15 days:

1st day: barber, doctor, showers
2nd day: beans instead of broad beans for lunch (Epiphany)
3rd day: we saw my mother for five minutes
5th day: we got two parcels from my mother
7th day: distribution of oranges
10th day: visit of the English Consul
11th day: change of cell
15th day: distribution of figs, oranges

Such are the events that mark a prisoner: most of them concern his stomach.

4) Personal reflections

Having nothing else to do in prison, a lot of time is devoted to thought.

There is always a lot of noise everywhere; it is continuous, from morning to night.

The man at the head of the black-market is called the "*medico*" (doctor).

The guardiens know only four words: "*todos*" (all there);

"venga" (go); *"anda"* (quickly) and *"mañana"* (tomorrow). After a few days in prison, you start to await the usual events of the day with a certain impatience.

If you want to really appreciate the joys of a normal life I can only recommend that you try to get locked up for a month.

MORE PRISON LIFE

As I have mentioned, on the eleventh day of our imprisonment we were put in another cell. We were still with the four people we had met in the frontier village and now two of them, the Meyer brothers from Luxemburg, who had become our friends, were released. Apparently into some kind of house arrest in the city – it was never very clear, even though we met them long after, in London.

We were transferred to cell 85 on the first floor where the four of us stayed together for another two days. Then the authorities decided to put all the English together (a few more had arrived) and four others joined us, replacing the Officer and the Austrian Jew who had accompanied us so far. All four of these new arrivals were English agents who had been parachuted into France on sabotage missions. Shortly afterwards, three of them left us to be put under house arrest and they were replaced by two children, seventeen and fifteen years old, who had just crossed the border all alone.

There was also a Frenchman in the prison, who had also crossed the border illegally but who did not seem to want to leave. He acted as interpreter for the authorities and therefore enjoyed a privileged existence. It was a matter of public notoriety that he was the prison informer and nobody spoke to him voluntarily.

One of our best friends was the prisoner with whom we had spoken to on the first day. He was a big man and was condemned for life. He spoke a little French and since he had been in jail since the civil war, he was left to do more or less what he liked. According to the snatches of conversation which we were able to get with him and with others, he was known as the "Butcher of Murcie" because he executed nationalists during the civil war.

On January 24th, we learned that the American Red Cross was going to make a big distribution of warm clothes, blankets, chocolate and oranges. The distribution did take place but was initially somewhat disappointing as it consisted of a pair of fur-lined gloves for everyone. Soon, however, this was supplemented by warm underclothes, blankets, chocolate, oranges and condensed milk and it went a long way to improve our standard of living for the few days which we still had to undergo at Pamplona Provincial Prison.

A FORETASTE OF FREEDOM, A ROCK AND EN ROUTE FOR
ENGLAND

On 26th January, 22 days after our imprisonment, we were released at the same time as the only other English prisoner in the PPP. We had just finished our lunch, at 1 pm, when the "Butcher of Murcie" informed us that we were free: "completely free" were the words he used. He seemed as happy as we were about it and embraced me as if to prove it. We were so overjoyed that we forgot to say goodbye to the guard on the last gate as we left. A taxi was waiting for us outside and we jumped in without paying attention to anything else. A few hundred yards further on I turned to look through the back window and realised that we were being followed by another car carrying a British number plate. It was only then that we really believed it was really happening and not just another Spanish lie.

The Consul himself was waiting at the Police station and after some very brief formalities, he took us to an hotel for lunch and left telling us he would be back at five fifteen to take us to the station for the five thirty train. We had already lunched in prison, but it was with great pleasure that we repeated the operation. Afterwards we went into the city to look at the shops and to eat cakes, not only to kill time and hunger, but just out of sheer pleasure at being able to do whatever we wanted.

As planned, the Consul came to pick us up, ran us to the station at top speed and put us on the train. There was hardly time to give us our instructions before the train left. The trip was not very comfortable especially as we were inspected at least six times and that the last inspector told us that we should have been accompanied by somebody from the consulate. In view of this, when we arrived in Madrid, we just took time to kiss my mother, who was on the platform, and then left as quickly as possible, grabbing a taxi to take us to the consulate.

My mother had arrived in Madrid two or three days after her imprisonment and on her arrival, because all the public offices were closed for the weekend, had to spend another three days in jail, this time at the Central Madrid Prison.

We stayed in Madrid six days. It was six days of rehabilitation for me; not because of the prison, it was something deeper than that, a kind of apprenticeship for a different way of life, a complete re-education. No more worrying about the Gestapo, no more watching your tongue, able to go anywhere, and no more of that all pervading German propaganda. One of our best memories of that short stay in Madrid was that we were made honorary members of the Anglo-American club (which had a collection of sherries, the like of which I have never seen) and it was there that we spent a good part of our time. Another was an invitation to dinner by an embassy attaché at his home. And, of course, we could go wherever we wanted, do whatever we liked.

Here are some notes on my stay in Spain:

In the five weeks I was there, I did not meet a single Franco supporter. The Spanish army, built on the model of the German army, changed the guard in front of the dictator's palace with military band and bagpipes. One of the Meyer brothers, who had lived in Spain, had told us that anyone could live there as long as he knew three Spanish words: *"Dormire"* (to sleep); *"Comer"* (to eat) and *"Retrete"* (toilet).

I have never seen a piece of paper as disgusting as a Spanish banknote. In the elections before the civil war, there were just 7,000 communists in Spain. But what men: it took Franco two years, with half of Spain on his side, a powerful army and German and Italian equipment to overcome the communists.

Three observations about the siege of Madrid:

- The centre of the city was never bombarded because it was the residential district of the Generals.
- The defenders of Madrid travelled by tram to lunch at home.
- A football match was organised between the lines and between the two enemies: it ended in the victory of the defenders by 4 goals to 2

After this pleasant stay in the Spanish capital, we left Madrid for Gibraltar the following Monday.

A large rock, a port full of boats, an aerodrome where the racecourse had been, a small city with crowded houses lower down but which spread out from each other, further and further, as one climbed the rock. That's about all there is to Gibraltar. We arrived there on Tuesday afternoon after a tiring but picturesque trip of some twenty hours.

You would have to have seen the Spanish trains to believe what I have to say about them. They must have been the oldest trains in existence; from Madrid to

Algéciras (the last station before Gibraltar) it was single track railway which one would have thought would have involved delays for trains in the other direction. This wasn't a problem: there weren't any. At each station the driver would get into conversation with the station master and sometimes have a card game with him, this was probably to encourage local trade which consisted of a horde of dirty children who descended upon us, offering oranges and figs for sale. And what a delicious fruit the fig is. In prison it was the only thing one could get to improve the diet: dried figs. I gather they are very good for the stomach but unfortunately, there are other parts of the human anatomy for which they are less beneficial. Try eating dried figs for a month at the rate of one every fifteen minutes and see what happens.

This said, let us return to our muttons. In Algéciras, we were put in three buses, which took us to La Linea, where our papers were once again checked and from where we left for the free world. On our way we passed anti-tank barrages, crossed trenches, went over a canal and stopped at the gate to Gibraltar. There, a customs officer asked us if we had cameras, alcohol or firearms and, given a negative answer, allowed us to enter. And there, in all his splendid majesty, a British police officer, in familiar uniform, opened the passage to freedom for us.

My mother was once again separated from us because women were prohibited on the Rock. She had to go to the hospital while we were placed in a small hotel in Main Street. As soon as we had claimed our rooms we went back into the street and found a café where we could get a decent beer. Gibraltar Main Street was a curious sight in the evening: hundreds, if not thousands of soldiers, sailors and airmen, from all parts of the world, were walking around in groups with nothing to do. The military police walked in wary groups of six, looking out for fights.

After dinner, we went up to our room, which at that moment was being subjected to an invasion of ants whose columns converged on our oranges: a substantial battle ensued, which we eventually won but with losses on both sides, amounting to three oranges on ours.

The following day, we rose early and were having our breakfast when the owner of the hotel announced that a taxi was waiting for us. As we had so often done before, we threw our things together in a few moments and left for the port. In less than half an hour we were aboard the boat and had already learned that it had no alcohol on board, nor, for that matter, any drink stronger than tea.

Making the best of it we went on deck to await my mother, who arrived at two o'clock and at four the boat left the quay to anchor in the port. The sight of Gibraltar at night was really splendid because not only did it not have a blackout but the searchlights, which criss-crossed the sky, added drama to the picture. The next morning, we were on the open sea.

We were in a convoy of ten troopships, escorted by two corvettes and an aircraft carrier. We spent seven days on board, the food was first class and everything was done to relieve the monotony of the voyage.

On 9th February, we anchored in the Clyde, in Scotland.

HOMECOMING

I have never been so happy to see the British coast as on that morning of 9th February. I do believe what most affected me was the sight of a red double-decker bus driving along the coast road. After a few formalities on the boat, we set foot on British soil and were free for the first time in three and half years.

We immediately left for Edinburgh, where we had friends, and stayed there the following day. I bought myself a hat there, partly because the beret is rarely worn in Britain (I was still wearing the one I had bought in Pau) and partly to hide my Pamplona haircut.

That same evening, we left for London and we arrived at my grandmother's as the clock struck nine.

It may seem odd but I was always struck by the frequency with which the figure seven cropped up during our adventures; Tuesday is the only day of the week with seven letters and the letter G is the seventh of the alphabet. It was on Tuesday that we left prison, the next Tuesday we entered the British Empire, where? Gibraltar, and the next Tuesday we entered the Clyde where we disembarked at Gourock (seven letters), from where we left for Glasgow (seven letters). Since we had left Lyon on the 18h 18 train on December 23rd, and that we arrived at my grandmother's at 9 o'clock on 11th February, our entire trip took forty-nine days, fourteen hours and forty two minutes – all divisible by seven.

And now, most of our sufferings were over and I could start to think of the time when I would be able to return to Paris – but in different circumstances. In the meantime at least we were in a free country, where, in spite of the war and all its troubles, people wore a smile on their faces and kept their sense of humour. Like those two soldiers in their tent, woken in the middle of the night by a huge explosion:

1st Soldier: "What was that? Thunder, or a bomb"?

2nd Soldier: "A bomb".

1st Soldier: "Thank God, I thought it was going to rain again".

"J'ai Vécu la Guerre"

Renée Simonet

A conversation with Madame Renée Simonet, aged 88, in which she movingly recounts, with no little emotion, but with the utmost clarity, some of her memories of living in Paris as a teenager under the Occupation.

"Oui, j'ai vécu la guerre. (Yes, I lived through the war). I was only 15 when the Germans arrived in Paris. I was 20 when they left. I had to leave school because I had to go out and work. We were very poor and the family needed the money. We ate very badly. We survived on bread, potatoes and turnips with carrots as a special treat when they were available. There was no meat or fish in Paris in those days.

There was only a minimum of public transport. I went everywhere by bicycle and on foot. So I suppose I was quite fit, but I was always terribly hungry. A young teenager needs food. Yes there were times when we went without meals. Of course there was a black market, but the prices were beyond our reach. There were never any fat Frenchmen or women during the war. There were a few fat, desk-bound Germans. But the German soldiers had themselves known shortages in the late 1930s at home. When they arrived in Paris they bought up all the chocolate they could lay their hands on.

Do you know what my happiest day in the war was?

It was my birthday in 1945, the very same day when it was announced that Chancellor Hitler was dead. (I am very proud that I was born in the same month as Queen Elizabeth II). That man stole my youth.

I am too old now to be bitter, and I suppose that at the age of 88 I can say that I am healthy today, despite those war-time privations. I went out with a G.I., but I didn't accept his proposal and go back to the States with him. So I am a life-long Parisian, the city I love. But I still have unhappy memories of those dark days . . . "

As reported to Roger Thorn, by way of a brief face-to-face interview in October 2013.

Arrival at Belsen

Jean-Pierre Renouard

The gate closes behind us, but not a single SS guard enters with us. We are surrounded by a group of young Soviets who were obviously expecting us, as they immediately start searching us and taking everything we've brought from Misburg, mainly our potatoes and our fish. The camp is ill lit, and you can barely make out the huts. The Soviets point out to us one with an open door, and we go in. It is appalling. There is nothing and no one is here, no barrack boss, no bunks, no pallets – nothing but a handful of pale beings stretched out on the bare floor. They don't even seem to notice us. The floor is covered with human waste and scraps of clothing.

I explore a bit and finally come up with a garden spade, which I bring back to the hut. We use it to shovel up some of the filth and clear a space where we can try to sleep. But I see that one of my comrades from Misburg has been knocked down and is being beaten by the Soviets, who are trying to take his rubber boots. I lift the shovel and start swinging at random. The Russkies run off, some of them with bloody heads. We dig away all the muck we can, more or less clearing an area a couple of yards square. We go to sleep practically on top of one another. I sleep sitting with my back to the wall, the spade near at hand.

In the early morning at first light, I go looking for the toilets. They exist all right, but they are full of corpses, stacked up to the ceiling. All the dead are skeletal. I relieve myself, my eyes riveted on what were once men, men who laughed and ran and loved. In the middle of the pile is a pair of eyes that are not glassy like the others. One of the skeletons is looking back at me. He's been lying here, with the others piled on top of him, for God knows how long. But he is not yet dead.

I hasten to rejoin my comrades, and we go outside. Things are just the same there. There are corpses everywhere. There's a pile behind the hut, another here, another there. We even see two men, too weak to stand up, crawling along on all fours and occasionally exchanging a few words. I set out to see whether there isn't, somewhere in the camp, somebody distributing something to eat.

THE CAMP

I contemplate the scene. Bergen-Belsen is a big camp, with scores of huts, surrounded by a thick forest that starts just a few yards past the thick barbed-wire fence and stretches off into the distance. It's in a kind of natural clearing, far from any civilian settlement. The site was well chosen for starving large numbers of people to death. I recall that when we arrived at Neuengamme, the SS officers ordered the old, the sick, and the feeble to fall out so that they could be sent to a camp where they would not have to work. They no doubt came here, for it's not far away from Neuengamme. They all must have died long ago.

A main road starts at the gate and runs straight through the camp, dividing it in two. The men's barracks seem to be mostly on the left. They are built of wood, with cracked paint, dilapidated and dirty. There are some large buildings on the right, one of them apparently the camp kitchen. There seems to be no organization here, just gangs of Soviets who exercise *de facto* control of the camp. Some inmates don't even have striped uniforms. They're wearing the same civilian clothes they had on when they were arrested. Later I learn that they are Jews from Central Europe.

THE WOMEN'S CAMP

Along the main camp road, there's an SS guard standing alongside a large handcart. A couple of inmates wait nearby. The guard yells at me to join the detail, and we set off, dragging the empty cart. The guard opens a gate in a barbed-wire fence, and we enter the women's camp. The path is winding, and the huts are set back from it among young trees. At various points along the edge of the path are piles of naked female corpses piled up like logs, just as in the men's camp. We load some in the cart. When it is full, we return to the central road and head for the far end of the camp, some of us pushing, some pulling our heavy load.

The guard tells us to stop, and we manoeuvre the cart to the rim of a large pit, some thirty feet deep, which is already half full of corpses tossed in any old way. There are already a considerable number of them. By now, I don't even notice the smell of death that hangs everywhere. Once the cart is empty, we return to the women's camp and fill it up again. I make the same trip, back and forth, all day long, without stopping, without drinking or eating anything.

At a certain point, as we approach, a group of women emerges from one of the huts carrying a young girl's body wrapped in a blanket. They weep as they hand it over to us with elaborate care. They try to tell us how wonderful the dead girl was. We exchange a few words in German. To cheer them up a little, I tell them that I am an American and that the Allied troops will be arriving very soon. Their faces light up and they slip me some bread, which I hide under my shirt. I have often thought that I may have carried the body of Anne Frank to her grave.

I'm outside, with Father Leroy.

"I won't tell the others," he says, "but I can say this to you. I just don't understand how God allows such horrors to go on, how He can look on and not intervene."

"But, father," I reply, "you forget that there have always been such horrors and that God has always stood by. I don't want to offend you, but you certainly recall that the Spaniards killed millions of Indians in Latin America and completely destroyed their ancient civilizations in the very name of Jesus Christ."

"Yes, it's probably true. But they thought they were doing the right thing. They thought they were converting pagans, saving their souls."

"Everyone always thinks he's doing the right thing. By the way, I wonder whether the German soldiers still have the old motto "Gott mit uns" – God with us – engraved on their belt buckles, like the Kaiser's soldiers did. I haven't looked. And besides, father, you know there's the Kingdom of God and the kingdom of man, and that they're not the same kingdom at all."

"I don't understand you," Father Leroy says. "You find all this normal. But I'm shocked that the Nazis, who are Europeans and should be civilized people after all, can behave the way they do here and elsewhere."

"We were in the Resistance, father, don't forget that. We were fighting them. Remember what we called ourselves: 'soldiers without uniforms.' They had every right to shoot us on the spot. Yet now, after a whole year in the camps, after everything they've made us go through, we're still standing up. Not very strong, I admit, but standing up. When I think of all our comrades who have already died, I guess we shouldn't complain too much. Besides: complain to whom, who cares? The only thing to do is shut up and go on as long as we can, hoping we can make it to the end. That's all."

That evening, I return to the men's camp and share my bread with Jean Gambier, Sergio de Navarro, and Ernst Pinxter. I've been with the last two from way back, since well before Compiègne, before Neuengamme and Misburg. Sergio is a splendid fellow. I met him when they marched us out of prison and packed us into a freight car at Bordeaux. He is a Spaniard. Sergio's father was mayor of Barcelona during the Spanish civil war and took his family across the border when Barcelona fell to Franco. Sergio was arrested in Toulouse one night when he was bicycling down the landing strip of a German air base, God knows why. He was dressed like a zoot-suiter: long jacket, tight trousers, white socks, and triple-soled shoes. He loved life, girls, and jazz. He was always good humoured. Now he's just a shadow of his former self.

Ernst is a young Dutchman from a prominent family who was arrested trying to cross the border between France and Spain to join Allied forces. He's intelligent, cultivated, and refined. He has a huge, sloping brow that is impressive.

Night falls, and the Soviets herd us all towards a hut with triple-decker bunks all the way around the walls. There's a narrow corridor in the middle, leading to the door. They lock us up in absolute darkness. I'm stretched out near Jean, Sergio and Ernst. We hear Paul groaning. Paul was with us at Misburg and before that in the port city of Kiel, where the German navy had him digging up unexploded Allied bombs. He's an engineer, so one day when the German bomb squad was late, he disarmed a bomb all by himself, thereby frightening hell out of everyone on the scene. Now, though, Paul is at the end of his rope. He's dying at the other end of the hut. He groans and calls for help, but there's nothing we can do for him. Here we are, four of his closest friends, stretched out in the dark, silent, open eyed, listening to him and absolutely powerless. Paul must have disturbed his neighbours. They haul him out of his bunk and throw him down in the corridor, where he goes on moaning, only more softly. In the morning, he's dead. His clothes are stripped off and he is thrown onto a pile with a few others who, unlike him, died in silence.

After the war, I attended a memorial service for Paul in Lyon. I shook hands with his parents, his relatives, his friends, his colleagues. I did not tell them about the way he died.

THE STOLEN RUTABAGAS

The camp appears to be out of the line of battle, for the sound of gunfire is infrequent and far away. I have no idea how the Allied troops are doing, and I'm beginning to worry. Since I arrived, no soup or bread has been handed out in the men's camp. That's why I go along every morning with the body-cart crew to the women's camp, where there's sometimes a scrap or bread to be had. But after a few days I can't take it anymore. If I go on doing this, I won't be able to look at a woman for the rest of my life without thinking of all those corpses.

So I stay in the men's camp with my friends from Misburg. From where we are, we can see a pile of rutabagas about six feet high on the other side of two rows of barbed wire. Between the wires there's a kind of corridor, along which an SS guard marches back and forth.

We count the seconds out loud, Jean Gambier, Sergio, Ernst, and I, in order to determine the exact time between the guard's rounds, and we decide to steal some rutabagas. We find an iron bar about three feet long, twist one end, and sharpen it. We find two jackets that still have buttons on them and fashion them into sacks, and we rip up the clothes of dead inmates to make rags. Each of us is assigned a task. Sergio and Ernst, who are very weak, will stay near the barbed wire and fill the sacks. Jean will pull open the wires, using the rags to protect his hands, and I, taking the greatest risk, will go through the fence into the corridor, where I will spear the rutabagas with the iron bar and throw them to my comrades. We pull it off once, then twice. The other inmates start to do the same, jumping into the corridor in a disorderly and disorganized way.

The guard, who for some unknown reason has turned around unexpectedly, screams at us, raises his rifle, cocks it, and takes aim. There are three of us in the corridor, ten yards away from him. I see the tiny black hole at the end of the rifle barrel pointing at me. I'm paralyzed. The shot goes off. The guy next to me falls. Somehow, I scramble back through the wire and mingle with my friends. I'm no longer in danger, but I'm stunned by the after effects of fear. I'm flat on the ground, unable to move or speak or think, pissing in my pants. It takes me a good fifteen minutes to recover, with my friends gathered around and making fun of me the whole time. Then we eat. We have enough rutabagas to hold out for a week.

THE CHAPLAIN DIES

Rutabagas are truly awful to eat, but they are all we have. Jean Gambier, as usual the most refined of us all, smokes his daily ration of rutabagas, spearing them on a sharp stick and turning them over a fire made of old clothes. It's a weird way to cook. I come along while he is in the midst of his smoking routine.

He says: 'If you sit down, I'll slug you!"

I am surprised, and he explains: "Look there, on the ground. You see Gaston, the old farmer from Brittany. He came along just like you. He sat down, we talked about Misburg for a while, and then he stopped talking, I looked, and he was dead. It took him one second to die, no death rattle, no jerk, no nothing. Poof. Then Gaston's son comes along. Then it's Father Leroy, our dear old chaplain, and the same story again. So if you don't mind, please just keep standing up."

I remain standing, thinking about these three men, all from the same region of France, who have stuck together for more than a year. They were together in prison in France, then at Compiègne, at Neuengamme, and at Misburg, and together they arrived here, at the end of the road. They died one after another only a few minutes apart, and now they're together on the other side. Probably watching us.

TYPHUS

I notice that the SS guards always stick to the roads, the main road that cuts through the camp and the one in the women's camp. I mention this to a guy who looks like he has been here for a while. He tells me there's typhus in the camp, that you get it from fleas, and that it's usually fatal. That is why there's no sign of a formal camp hierarchy.

He adds, "I'll catch it, you'll catch it, it's a matter of days. Nobody can escape it. You mustn't think about it. Thinking does no good."

The Allies had better get here fast. Otherwise, they won't find anyone left alive. So it turns out after all that these skeletal men and women didn't all die of starvation. Many of them died of typhus or some other epidemic.

A COMRADE

I'm sitting on the ground behind the huts, in a large area littered with corpses. A guy I knew at Misburg who doesn't like me show up.

He calls out: "So there you are, you shit! I thought you dropped dead long ago!"

I reply: "No, I'm still here, as you can see. But don't worry, it won't be long:" He laughs out loud and walks away.

A RUSSIAN DIES

The women's camp is not the only place that the SS want to clear of corpses before the Allied troops arrive. There is also the men's camp. But there is no handcart. So early one morning, the guards herd us out, along with the Soviets. We move the bodies one by one, dragging them feet first, four inmates for each cadaver, one man for each arm and each leg. We form a long, surrealistic parade stretching from the first huts to the pit, and the parade lasts all day long. It is a pure waste of time, for completing the task would take weeks.

During one of these macabre trips, I'm tugging a right leg when a Russian, who is supposed to be pulling the left leg, falls behind. I start to shout at him. The Russian looks at me and drops dead. In an instant, like Gaston, like Father Leroy, like so many others. Now I understand why he didn't have enough strength to pull his share a minute ago. It seems there were fifteen thousand bodies still unburied when the British troops arrived. Yet we really worked hard. I can even say that I did nothing but move bodies for almost two weeks.

POW

From where I sit, I can see the SS guards outside the camp, on the other side of the fence. Some are going in and out of various buildings and loading cars. Obviously, they are about to clear out. Others, however, seem not to care about this scurrying and go on with their usual tasks. On their right arms these men are wearing white armbands, with the letters POW painted in black. I look at them with puzzlement, and then, in a flash, I understand. POW must mean "prisoner of war." These men don't feel like getting shot at. They have surrendered in advance. Our brave SS guards. They were so impressive until now.

I have wondered since whether the SS negotiated with the British command to keep us locked up in order to avoid spreading the camp diseases all over Europe, especially typhus. Everybody knows how much the British hate communicable diseases, whether it be cholera in India during the Raj or rabies today.

I now know that it is true.

THE HUNGARIANS

At about this time, I notice soldiers in yellow-brown uniforms. They replace the SS in supervising us as we drag corpses to the mass grave. They are Hungarians, doubtless troops loyal to Horthy, the Hungarian regent, who has played an ambiguous game throughout the war, both supporting and resisting Hitler. God only knows how these men got here. But they blindly obey orders.

One afternoon, after an exhausting day, a number of us are heading back down the main road towards the first set of huts. We come face-to-face with a young Hungarian who is obviously frightened by this crowd of living ghosts spilling around him on all sides. He shouts orders in his own language, but we pay no attention. Then this idiot panics and shoots at us. The two inmates ahead of me fall, one after the other. But I'm unharmed. The bullet was stopped by the second man. Then our group surges forward and the Hungarian runs away. We move slowly towards the huts, leaving the two bodies in the road. Two more.

LIBERATION

On April 15, I'm on the camp road, returning from the pit, when I hear a kind of dull roar. In the distance I see an armoured vehicle with an officer on top, carrying a loudspeaker and saying I don't know what in several languages. He is a British officer. I look ... and look again. It's hard to believe. Finally!

I sit down and hold my head in my hands. I want to cry and to laugh. I stay this way for a good while, and then I continue toward the front of the camp. The inmates I pass seem unconcerned about what is happening. For many, for most of them, it is already too late. I follow a crowd of inmates, obviously looking for foot, to a warehouse, where the door has been knocked down and the contents are being looted. There's nothing here but military clothing. I find a pair of felt-lined boots that fit me. I slip them on after discarding the old pieces of ripped-up blanket I have been using as Russian footcloths as well as my disgusting shoes.

I return to the main road to see the arrival of a small column of British soldiers, rifles at the ready and an officer in the lead. They look enormously healthy and muscular by comparison with us. I remove my hat, stand to attention, and offer them my services as an interpreter. By now, I speak and understand enough German and Russian to do this job, at least for a while.

The British officer replies that, unfortunately for me, he doesn't need any help. His men are part of a fighting unit and he's going to leave soon for the front. He adds: "Besides, you won't be leaving this camp for several weeks. We need time to get organized. There's typhus here, and we don't want to be responsible for an epidemic. We have only one paramedic for sixteen men. And he has what he needs to treat wounds, but no diseases." How unprepared they are!

I don't want to stay here any longer. I plead my case, but to no avail. Finally I say, "My mother is British, her maiden name was Padwick. Before she married my father, who is a Frenchman, she lived on Carlisle Road, in Eastbourne, Sussex."

This is a whopping lie: Mrs. Padwick ran a boarding-house where I spent a vacation before the war.

But it works. The officer says: "Okay, be at the camp gate this evening, and you can leave. Meanwhile, show me what there is to see here."

To see! My God!

I lead the British patrol to the edge of the pit. It isn't yet filled to the brim, far from it. But there are already thousands of bodies. The British soldiers stay there for a moment, petrified with horror, and then begin to swear. Some of them turn away to vomit.

With tears in his eyes, the officer says, "I've been fighting this war for four years, and I haven't seen anything as horrible as this. I didn't think anything like this could even exist."

As for me, I had stopped paying attention a long time ago.

SERGIO DIES

A mass of staggering inmates appears to be heading for a kind of field surrounded with barbed wire. Once there, they begin digging in the ground. Under little heaps of straw, there are potatoes. I tuck my jacket into my trousers and tighten the string that serves as my belt. I fill my jacket with potatoes, carefully buttoning it up for fear that some may fall out.

I meet Sergio on the way back to camp. I ask him for news of the others. He tells me that Ernst has died quietly and that he's lost tract of Jean Gambier, who still seemed to be all right. As for Sergio himself, he's near the end, looking like a ghost. I lead him to a hut, clean out a bunk, and tuck him in under three blankets, hiding some of my potatoes under his feet. I break up some boards and build a fire outside the hut on which to cook the rest of the potatoes. I watch the fire. I watch Sergio. He smiles, wanly. I speak to him. He doesn't seem to hear. The wood has burned down to charcoal. I place my potatoes carefully on the coals. I go back into the hut. Sergio is dead.

I go out. I wonder what I'm doing still on my feet while my friends are all dying, one after the other.

Why them and not me?

LUNCH

There's a guy squatting by the fire, looking at my potatoes. He says, "You have potatoes, I have some meat, let's share." I agree. He goes off to get his meat and comes back to cook it. Suddenly I understand.

"Where did you get that meat?"

He laughs but doesn't answer.

"That has to be human flesh. I don't want any. Keep it. And I'll keep my potatoes."

He becomes furious and threatening: "You agreed to share. You can't change your mind. Even if you don't want any of my meat, you have to give me half of your potatoes."

Such is concentration camp logic. I snatch a brand out of the fire and hit him in the face with it. He runs off, screaming.

Then a woman appears, young and frail looking. She stares at my potatoes.

I ask her, in German, "Who are you?"

She replies, "A Jew."

"No, that's not what I meant. What is your nationality?"

"Austrian."

"Well, starting right now, when someone asks you, you have the right to say that you're Austrian. Please sit down and share these potatoes with me."

We leave the meat on the fire until it burns down to charcoal.

I LEAVE

Evening falls. I head for the camp gate. I catch sight of the British officer I talked to this morning and call to him. He comes to the gate, speaks to the soldiers on guard, and I walk out. Without regrets. I'm not abandoning anyone. My friends are almost all dead. I must weigh ninety or one hundred pounds, but I'm still standing. I no longer notice my repulsive filthiness or my fleas. I even have the feeling I'm quite elegant in my felt-lined boots, but I do notice that the officer keeps a fair distance between us. We go to the SS barracks, now occupied by British soldiers, in whose care the officer leaves me. He goes off, wishing me good luck.

Within myself, I feel very strong. I'm hardened, ready for anything, capable of anything. For a whole year I've worked under constant blows. I've been starved and deprived of sleep. I've been so cold I shivered from head to toe for weeks on end. I've been sick and not been treated. And I've survived.

I leave the concentration camp world believing my troubles are over. For the moment, all I can think about is eating. I am only vaguely aware that I'm going to have to unlearn everything I've learned in the camps if I am to return to civilization.

I'm not so sure that I want to.

MASS GRAVES

The pit at the end of the camp, now only half full, will be filled to the rim in the days and weeks following the camp's liberation. Other pits will be dug and filled with the skeletal bodies of wretched men and women from many countries, of many religions and nationalities. There will be no way for the British to identify them. A total of five thousand, maybe ten thousand or more, no one knows.

All across Europe, as month follows month, mothers, fathers, wives, sisters, whole families will gradually lose all hope of ever seeing their loved ones again. Then, finally, they will accept their loss. Peace be with them.

Part 3: Servicemen and Women

serv·ice·man
[sur-vis-man, -muhn]

noun, plural serv·ice·men [sur-vis-men, -muhn] .

a member of the armed forces of a country.

also called (feminine): servicewoman a person who serves in the armed services of a country

Origin:
1920–25; service + man

Churchill's Secret Army

Noreen Riols

The following comes from Noreen Riols' recent book
The Secret Ministry of Ag & Fish. *Noreen Riols was a
member of the secretive Special Operations Executive
(S.O.E.), and her role was to assist in the preparation
and training of the Agents who would subsequently
work behind the lines as Winston Churchill's "Secret
Army". Hers is amongst the more unusual of the stories
to be told, illuminating as it does what has until recent
times been very much a closed and secretive world.*

My mother thought I worked for the Ministry of Ag.
and Fish.

She died without ever knowing the truth. And she
wasn't the only one. Because all those who worked for
Churchill's Secret Army were under the Official Secrets
Act and it wasn't until 2000, after sixty years, that
the government opened S.O.E. files to the public, and
immediately the media pounced on we few survivors
who were still upright - well, more or less! "How were
you recruited?" "Why were you recruited?" "Who
proposed you?" they asked. I'd really like to know. Even
today, after almost seventy years I still have no idea
who recruited me or why.

On reaching the ripe old age of seventeen my call-
up papers arrived: join the armed forces or work in
a munitions factory! The latter option did not appeal

so I decided to join the Womens' Royal Naval Service, the "Wrens": because I liked the hat. But when I went to enlist, a vinegar-faced woman told me the only vacancies were for cooks and stewards. Spending the war making stew and suet pudding was not the way I'd imagined myself leading my country to victory. "It's that or a munitions factory", Vinegarface threatened. "Make up your mind".

I didn't make up my mind. Vinegarface did. She put me down for a factory. "I will not work in a factory", I stamped, puce with rage.

A door opened and a man in uniform walked out "I'll take over this case, Miss Hoskins", he said tersely, holding out his hands for my file and ushering me into his office. "I see you've just left the Lycée Francais", he remarked studying my papers.

I refrained from adding that I hadn't had any choice. "So you speak French ... "

"And Spanish, and German," I snapped, still seething. He began shooting questions at me, leaping about in four languages like a demented kangaroo. He seemed surprised that I was able to keep up. After a few more linguistic gymnastics, he made a mysterious telephone call and sent me to 64 Baker Street. Ah, I thought, now I'm going to get my seductive hat. I couldn't have been more wrong. The plaque on the wall outside: "Inter-Services Research Bureau" didn't mean a thing. I think that was the idea. Like the hordes of other passers-by, I didn't realise or even suspect that this was in fact the Headquarters of the Special Operations Executive, Churchill's Secret Army. I doubt I even knew of the existence of such an army.

The colonel who received must have approved of me since he told me to go to a certain office where, according to him, Captain Miller was expecting me. He may have been, but when I arrived, he'd forgotten! He stared at me as if I'd dropped in from outer space and suddenly barked: "No-one, but no-one must know what you do here. Not your father, your mother, your sister, your brother, your fiancé."

I never discovered who else wasn't supposed to know. Before he had time to tick off a few more members of my family on his fingers, an Irish Guards officer exploded like a bomb into the room making extraordinary squeaking sounds: and the two of them roared off down the corridor.

A Major, sticking pins into a map on the wall, turned round and without further introduction said abruptly: "Don't ask questions. The less you know the less you can reveal if the worst happens." Then he went back to his pins.

I hadn't had a chance to open my mouth, much less ask questions and was beginning to wonder what could possibly be worse than being trapped in this madhouse. It turned out to be a German invasion. And we were all, apparently, on their "black list". But I learned that later!

I also learned later that Captain Miller and his Irish Guards chum had just returned from "the field" - the code name for enemy territory, everything was in code - and were still on edge. That was putting it mildly! Also that when escaping, the Irishman had been shot in the throat transforming him into a ventriloquist's doll. But that afternoon I was unaware of these details and was convinced I had been lured into a hyperactive lunatic asylum run by the Crazy Gang.

"Is it always like this?" I asked a young F.A.N.Y. sitting unperturbed at her desk, studying her finger nails. "No", she reassured me. "It's usually worse! You'll get used to it".

I did. I didn't have any option. I'd been press-ganged into becoming a member of Churchill's Secret Army, and entered a hidden world of secret agents on "special operations".

S.O.E. was a family, but an enclosed family, also enclosed on the inside. I discovered that representatives from every occupied country were also working in the building, organising sabotage and the infiltration at night of secret agents into enemy territory by fishing boat, felucca, submarine and parachute, but there was no contact between us. The secret was absolute.

I was sent to the largest section F, for France, headed by the now legendary Colonel Buckmaster. The section was composed of English, French and, like my children, "half and halfs". It was a living *"entente cordiale"*. We didn't have any hours off, sometimes we worked all night, and weekends didn't exist, we took a day off whenever we could.

Being part of Churchill's Secret Army was a thrilling, exhilarating life full of action . . . and emotion. We experienced some very intense moments. We knew all the F Section agents; they circulated endlessly in the corridors. Some had just returned from "the field" because they were "blown", code for "wanted by the Gestapo", or wounded when a Lysander, a light aircraft which could land in a small space was sent after nightfall to rescue them. A dangerous operation because once the plane crossed the Channel it was subject to German flak, and often shot down before reaching the target, or on the way back. These highly-trained pilots had to have at least 250 hours night flying time behind them before even being considered operational and were all under the Official Secrets Act. They were mostly very young, between 19 and 23. One I remember was 27. His comrades called him "Uncle" in deference to his "great age". They belonged to Squadrons 138 and 161, known in-house as the "Moonlight Squadron" because they flew without lights navigating by the moon following the course of rivers, villages, towns, churches and cathedral spires.

At a recent annual commemoration ceremony for the 104 F Section Agents who did not return, I witnessed a very moving, reunion. After 67 years, a wounded agent met the pilot who had flown in to rescue him.

"The last time I saw you," Bob reminisced, "was when your head shot out of the cockpit and you yelled: "Get him on board quick! The Germans are after us." He paused. "I'd trust my life with you today." Once fit, Bob parachuted again into France.

Other escaping agents crossed the Pyrenees at night, following a guide. Sometimes the guide betrayed them to the Spanish border police and they landed in Miranda or Lerida prisons, which were little more than concentration camps. But their training had taught the agents escape tactics, and how to wriggle out of handcuffs! It could take them six months to get back to England during which time we often didn't know whether they were alive or dead.

Harry Peulevé, a twenty four year old "half and half" broke both legs on landing. He was hidden, patched up by a local doctor sympathetic to the Resistance, then crossed the Pyrenees on two sticks. And those guides walked fast! Back in England he was hospitalised then also parachuted again into France. Those men had guts.

Other potential agents were leaving for Arisaig, or Group A, in the north of Scotland to begin their six month training - eight to nine months for a radio operator. Here they were subjected to a harsh physical regime to put them into tip top condition. They would need to be fit once "in the field". Crawling under barbed wire in pouring rain, leaping over walls, walking miles over mountains and rough territory carrying heavy backpacks, being dumped in the wilds and left to find their own way back, living off berries and whatever they could salvage from the countryside, learning to poach, shoot, map read, handle explosives, and kill the enemy... silently.

After Arisaig, they attended secret training schools dotted about the country: parachute, radio, sabotage, propaganda, use of arms, escape tactics, how to react under interrogation and torture, ending their training deep in the New Forest on Lord Montagu's estate at Beaulieu, Group B, where all the houses had been requisitioned for S.O.E. Beaulieu was known as the "finishing school for secret agents'" and was where they learned the art of spying. Only six women worked at Beaulieu during, the war and I believe I am the only survivor. I know I am the only woman survivor of F Section in France, together with four male agents, the youngest of whom is 89!

By the time the agents arrived at Beaulieu, some had formed romantic attachments. I remember at least three sets of agents who met and married before leaving for the field. Only one of these three couples survived the war, the other two perished in concentration camps. For security reasons they were not allowed to work together in the field. If captured by the Gestapo their feelings could blur their judgement, especially if one was tortured in front of the other in an attempt to break them and "encourage" them to "talk". Sometimes newly-married couples left on the same night from the same airstrip, but on separate planes for different destinations. Their goodbyes were heartbreaking.

Many women working for S.O.E. had their hearts broken, and I was no exception. It was at Beaulieu that at nineteen I fell madly in love. Our idyll lasted less than three months. Then Bill left, and didn't return; one of the many who disappeared without trace. All that remained was a sepia photograph and his last letter, given to me after he left. A little cameo of a perfect love: perfect because it was so brief. But for many women that cameo was all they ever had because their men did not return.

At Beaulieu, we women were used as "decoys" operating in nearby Bournemouth and Southampton, where the local population never suspected a thing!

We trained future agents to detect if they were being followed, taught them how to shake off their pursuer and how to follow a person without being detected. To pass messages without moving their lips or showing any sign of recognition. This last exercise often took place in telephone booths, on park benches and also in cafes and restaurants. A favourite place in Bournemouth, where I operated, was the café above the Gaumont cinema. I remember consuming endless toasted tea-cakes while waiting for, or trying to detect my "victim". It would have been awkward, to say the least, to pass a table and hiss a compromising message into the ear of a complete stranger, or to surreptitiously drop a note into his lap giving a rendezvous. Should I choose the wrong person I could have been taken into custody for soliciting!

But the most "James Bond" (his creator was an agent working for naval intelligence) exercise took place in two hotels in Bournemouth where we women were used, over dinner, to discover whether an agent was likely to "talk". Most of them didn't. The Brits were pretty tight-lipped. One I remember said he was on a boring course for the "War Box" another that he was a representative for toothpaste, which was ridiculous: we didn't have any toothpaste. We used soot or salt. But it was his story, and he stuck to it.

The foreigners sometimes talked, especially if they were young. I understood. They were lonely, far from their country and their families, not knowing whether they would even have a country or a family to return to when this dreadful was over. And it was flattering to have a young girl hanging on their every word. I always felt terrible afterwards having to denounce them ,knowing that by so doing I put their chances of leaving on a mission in jeopardy. They'd survived at least six months of rigorous training, and Beaulieu was no rest cure, and then through one simple slip on a moonlit evening they might not be allowed to leave.

I remember one young student in particular, a Dane, a gorgeous blond Adonis. After dinner I managed to persuade him to take a stroll on the terrace adjoining the dining-room, which overlooked the sea. Actually he didn't need a great deal of persuading. I think he was rather taken with me but I was younger then, weighed several kilos less, didn't have white hair or need glasses to read the small print! It was a beautiful spring evening. The moon was shining on the sea rippling on the sand below. It was all very romantic and he became sentimental, held my hand and asked me if we could spend the following Sunday together. I agreed, knowing full well that there was no way I could spend Sunday with him. But it gave me my cue, my lead in. I was able to probe further, ask him if that would be it, just one meeting or would we be able to meet again. He had mentioned he was leaving: where was he going? Was it far? Would he be away long etc? And finally he talked.

The day before prospective agents left Beaulieu to return to London where their fate was decided, each one was interviewed by Colonel Woolrych, the Commandant at Beaulieu. He had the reports from all the schools they had attended on his desk and, after studying them, wrote his assessment of the student's capabilities. If they had talked, the door would open, I would enter and Woolybags – we called him that behind his back – would say "Do you know this woman?"

Mostly they shrugged and took it well, although it must have been a bitter disillusionment and disappointment. But this Dane was different. The day after our rendezvous when, during his interview, I entered Woolybags' office a look of astonishment flashed across his face, followed by what I can only describe as an expression of pain. To be suddenly replaced by rage. He half-rose from his chair and spat: "You bitch!"

No woman likes to be called a bitch, and I was upset. But as Woolybags said afterwards: "If he can't resist talking to a pretty face over here he won't when he's over there, and then it won't be only his life he's putting in danger but many others." He was right. But this young Dane's anger only compounded the guilt I felt at having deceived him. Looking back now I realise that my whole life in S.O.E. was deception: a lie. I had to lie to my mother, to my friends. I lied to everyone outside "the racket", as S.O.E. was known in-house.

The final decision as to whether an agent should leave on a mission or not rested with the Head of Section. Buck, as we affectionately called Colonel Buckmaster, often said "they've learned their lesson. They won't do it again," and allowed them to go. But I don't know whether the heads of the other country sections were so understanding.

When agents left for the field, Buck or one of his assistants always accompanied them to the airport. They had dinner together and, when night fell, Buck walked with them to the waiting plane and gave them a parting present: a gold cigarette case, a pen or cufflinks for the men and a pen or gold powder compact for the women: "Just to let you know we shall be thinking of you," he used to say, adding, "you can always sell it if you're in a tight spot". He was at the airfield to say goodbye and he was there when they returned. I don't know when he slept.

Returning agents, brought back by the "Moonlight Squadron", arrived before dawn at Tempsford or Tangmere airports, then closed to the public, from which SOE operated. After a huge breakfast they were driven to London for debriefing since they could give valuable, often up-to-date information about life in occupied France. De-briefings, or "Y9"s as they were called, were conducted in Orchard Court, where SOE had a large flat occupying the whole of the first floor. And like the people of Southampton and Bournemouth, the other residents in the block never even suspected what was going on under their very noses!

I often accompanied the two interrogating officers to these "Y9"s, and the agent's different reactions were a revelation to me. Some were in a terrible state, nerves in shreds, shaking, chain smoking; others who appeared to have had much more traumatic experiences were calm and composed. I remember the day news arrived that Francis Cammaerts, one of our best agents, had been captured, condemned to death and was to be executed at dawn: he had a wife and two young children and F section was plunged in gloom. The following morning the news burst upon us: "Roger" (his code name) "has escaped". He was in hiding, with the Germans searching everywhere for him, so when night fell, a Lysander, or "Lizzie" as the pilots called them, was sent to fetch him. The following morning he walked into Orchard Court as cool as a cucumber, as if he'd spent the weekend sunbathing on a beach!

I realised then that we are all different, that every person has a different breaking point. It's not a question of courage or endurance. In dangerous or difficult situations, when faced with fear and torture, we can imagine but we cannot predict what our reactions will be. And our imagination can play us tricks. No-one can ever be sure of their breaking point: that moment when the body and spirit has reached the limit of human endurance and will crack. A number of these agents reached that moment.

The French called them "Les hommes de l'Ombre" - Men of the Shadows. We called them the Crosse and Blackwell Brigade because their badges bore the insignia "By appointment to His Majesty the King" the logo found on the Crosse and Blackwell pickle jars. Affectionately they were known as "Buck's Boys".

They were recruited from every branch of the Allied forces and were mostly between twenty and thirty five.

Only a few were approaching forty, one or two were even over forty, but they were the exception rather than the rule. They were young, courageous, motivated, often idealistic, and – looking back through sepia photographs – usually very handsome: and they were all volunteers. The élite of whatever country they represented. There were no advantages or privileges attached to joining S.O.E. They received the same pay as those of equal rank filing papers in a government office.

They knew they had a 50% chance of survival. In the beginning, a radio operator's life expectancy was six weeks! They also knew that once behind enemy lines, it would appear that an iron curtain had descended between them and England, cutting them off from home, country and family, unable either to send or receive personal messages. Their families in England, if there was a family, received an official card once a month stating: "We have news of your son/your husband. He is in good health". That's all. Nothing personal, no loving messages. But the agents, once infiltrated, did not even receive that.

They arrived in "the field" in civilian clothes without the protection of a uniform so, if arrested, they could not claim prisoner of war status. They were spies, and a spy's fate awaited them. They had false papers, a false name; everything about them was false. Before leaving, they had to absorb their cover story so that, if dragged from bed at three in the morning, drugged with sleep – and it often happened during their stay at Beaulieu, under fierce interrogation by Group B officers disguised as Gestapo with bright lights shining directly in their eyes dazzling them – they automatically repeated the details of their false identity. They literally became another person.

They were warned that if captured London could do very little for them, and before leaving, each agent was given an "L tablet" which was hidden on their person in a place of their choice. Men often asked to have it sewn behind the collar of their jackets, in the corner of a handkerchief, inside a pocket or lining. Some had hollow pipes in which they hid messages written on flimsy paper . . . and also the L tablet. One woman hid hers in a tube of lipstick!

If arrested by the Gestapo they were advised to swallow the tablet: it was cyanide, and would kill them within two minutes. But should they not take it, they were told not to "talk" for forty eight hours in order to give members of their "reseau" time to disperse and, hopefully, escape. A difficult order to obey when your finger and toenails are being pulled out one by one, electric shocks are shooting through your body, you are being subjected to the water treatment or suspended from the ceiling by your ankles or wrists and beaten senseless. But many did obey it.

Yeo-Thomas (who taught me to make ratatouille!), one of the most tortured of our agents, said that the first fifteen minutes were the worst. After three days, torture was easier to bear: the body became accustomed to pain. I'm not sure all agents would have agreed with him. Others said they whispered to themselves Shakespeare's sonnets, Bible verses, poems or counted up to one hundred over and over again in an attempt to divert their minds from the agony being inflicted on their bodies.

Agents were aware of all this before they left. They were warned. And they were afraid. I shared many confidences with departing agents. They told me of their fear of torture and of death, and I realised that brave men are always afraid: that courage is not the absence of fear, but the willingness to face fear and do the thing they fear. They faced their fears and left – many never to return.

I remember a Jewish radio operator who was going into France on a second mission. Two missions were not unusual: one agent parachuted into France seven times, another four. For a Jew to go at all was dangerous, yet many did go, but two missions as a radio operator, the most dangerous job of all, was almost suicidal. I spent the evening before he left with him. There was no romantic association: I was merely keeping him company. After all, he was an old man. He was thirty five! During the evening he took out of his pocket a velvet case in which was a gold chain holding a Star of David suspended above a dove of peace.

"I would like you to have this," he said simply.

I was embarrassed and didn't know what to say. "I'm very touched, but I couldn't possibly accept it," I finally stammered. He looked so disappointed. "Please do," he begged. "Oh, please do. My whole family in France has perished in a concentration camp. I have nobody left in the world and I'd like to think that someone remembers me: someone perhaps thinks of me when I am over there."

"In that case," I said, "I'll take it and look after it till you return." But he never returned.

We cannot know how many Allied soldiers lives were saved because of these lone commandos working behind the lines before D-Day, sending intelligence, reporting on enemy troop movements, recruiting and training the *maquis* and resistance groups into fighting units, sabotaging railway lines, blowing up bridges and arms dumps, dynamiting munitions factories to prevent the German army advancing. On his second mission into France on D-Day, Bob Maloubier, possibly F Section's greatest saboteur, blew up eight bridges. And he wasn't more than 23 at the time.

But we do know how many of our agents were captured, tortured, sent to concentration camps and executed, often in a horribly barbaric fashion, suspended on a wall by piano wire attached to a meat hook. Many were left to die an agonising death alone in a dark damp prison cell and countless others disappeared without trace, no doubt ending their lives as a pile of ashes outside the crematorium in an extermination camp like Flossenburg. Four women agents all under thirty were cremated alive at Natzweiler. They were given an injection which temporarily paralysed them, but the last one revived as she was about to be thrown into the flames and in an attempt to save herself from such a dreadful fate scratched the face of her executioner so badly that he bore the scars for the rest of his life.

"I was only an ordinary soldier doing my duty," he pleaded at his war crimes trial. Perhaps, but what a duty!

I had lunch a few years ago with three of the five remaining members of F Section in France. We three often used to meet to win the war all over again and were nicknamed *"les trois veterans et la gamine"* – "the three veterans and the kid (me!)".

One of the "veterans", Henri Diacono, a former radio operator who, shortly before his 21st birthday, had parachuted "blind" into France – without any reception committee waiting to receive him, was obliged to find his own way to his reseau. When I had known Henri in London during the war he was a curly-headed Frenchman. When we met again in 2000 during the making of a B.B.C. documentary that "curly-headed Frenchman" had very little hair left, he walked with a stick and sported a hearing aid!

"If you had the chance," he asked, turning to me during lunch, "would you do it again?"

"Would you?" I parried.

"I'm not sure," he reflected. "We were so young, weren't we? We didn't realise the danger."

It's true, at the time we were oblivious of danger. People were being killed every day all around us, but we thought we were immortal. The other two, who had both dropped twice from a moving plane on a moonlit night and drifted down to land in occupied France, agreed.

When France fell and practically the whole of Europe was in German hands Hitler, having Soviet Russia as his ally, was confident that the collapse of England was imminent, and a German invasion would be a mere formality. But he hadn't bargained for the bulldog spirit of Winston Churchill, that visionary who had predicted the threat of German aggression seven years earlier.

"We will never surrender", Churchill announced belligerently, in June 1940, his determination firing and inspiring the nation.

He called upon his close advisers to immediately organise a subversive army, a guerrilla force, responsible directly – and only – to him, which would cover every occupied European country and, working behind the Germans' back, carry out acts of sabotage and disrupt their means of communication. A secret hit and run army with the mission to "Set Europe ablaze" which, after the Navy, Army and Air Force would be his "Fourth fighting force". And S.O.E. was born.

But S.O.E. fought a war on three fronts. The official Intelligence Service MI6 disapproved of us. We didn't obey the conventional "rules" of war. Ours was a guerrilla war. So not only did S.O.E. have Germany as an enemy, but also MI6 and General de Gaulle. MI6 resented this "upstart" army composed of amateurs, and did everything in its power to frustrate and hinder S.O.E.'s efforts. They wanted to get rid of us. In this they were aided by General de Gaulle, head of his opposing organisation, the B.C.R.A. The general was a fiercely proud, patriotic, and one might say chauvinistic man who resented any interference by a foreign power in France's affairs. He appeared to have forgotten that France was a defeated country, now under the German boot. In an effort to wipe out S.O.E. and be solely responsible for organising clandestine operations in France he allied himself with MI6.

But S.O.E. was Churchill's brainchild, his "baby", and Churchill was the supreme authority. Since we were under his protection, not even the combined efforts of MI6 and General de Gaulle were able to remove us from the scene.

Churchill with his extraordinary vision understood that this war was going to be different from any other war Britain had ever fought. The age of gentlemanly warfare was over and MI6's soft shoe tactics would no longer work. To be victorious he needed a guerrilla army using subversive tactics, no holds barred. An army of "bandits". Which is what MI6 called us. "Amateur bandits". And they were right! We were bandits. That was our role, what Churchill intended us to be.

And we were amateurs. None of the agents intended making spying their career. They were all amateurs at the task they had undertaken, learning on the job. Lawyers, teachers, bankers, businessmen, wives and mothers who loved their country and had an ideal, a determination to fight the evil which had invaded Europe. And were prepared to follow their ideal, even unto death.

Amateur bandits, many of whom will not grow old as we who are left grow old, for they gave their today so that we might have our tomorrow.

The War

Whitmore George Hicks

Whitmore George Hicks' story is one encompassing many parts played in the War; a civilian trying to evade the occupying German forces, a member of the Resistance, and ultimately a British soldier. He endured a number of events and experiences which, with a relatively neutral tone, he committed into words for this account. Sadly he passed away some brief time before the completion of this book.

On Sunday 3rd September 1939 all the family, in the dining room at Vaucresson, were listening anxiously to the announcement of War declared on Germany. We all stood at attention whilst the National Anthem was played. The war had begun and I'm sure I didn't realise what war really meant.

Right at the beginning I filled in a form to join the army and was told to wait until I was called up. I was nearly 20 and could speak French perfectly so I thought I would be useful as an interpreter but nothing came from the British Embassy. In March I asked again and was told to fill in the same form and wait, or to go over to England at my own expense and join up from there. But I knew somebody who had done this and because he had come from France was refused. So I decided to carry on with my insurance job until I was called up.

In May the big German offensive started - Holland, Belgium, and the North of France. "They can't go on like that. Surely we are going to stop them," I thought. Then came the bombardment of Paris. At two o'clock in the afternoon, I was at the office, trying to watch from the attic. I heard a lot of planes and bombs but did not see anything. The first week of June we started evacuating the files from the office, just in case the Germans should come too close to Paris, were we to go to Nantes.

I went to spend the weekend with a girlfriend in Meulan (about 45kms North West of Paris). On Saturday evening and throughout the night, German planes were passing over us. On Sunday we learned that the Germans were about 90kms North East of us and we noticed a lot of evacuees on the road. Just after lunch a bridge over the river Seine, about 200 yards from us, blew up and we were ordered to evacuate the village, situated on an island, immediately. We started walking towards Paris pushing a canoe on wheels in front of us. We walked about ten miles on the road which was now a constant stream of evacuees. There were cars with mattresses on the top, horses and carts, bicycles, people walking and pushing prams or wheelbarrows full of luggage. At Villennes I was able to phone my father to tell him I would not be back that night. Luckily we had a friend in Villennes who put us up for the night. During the night two bombs fell a couple of hundred yards from the house. On Monday morning we managed to get a train for Paris. There I found out that my boss, Mr. H.R. Sprinks, had gone to Nantes, to where the office was evacuated. My father's office had also been transferred to Nantes.

We left our house at Vaucresson the following day, taking with us in the car my aunt and cousin. My sister, Joan, had gone with our aunt and uncle Blichlé to Brittany. My brothers Jack and Bob, and myself were to follow the car on our bicycles. When we left on the Tuesday evening, I thought everything would be alright, that we would get to Nantes in 3 or 4 days, and we could settle there until the Germans were pushed back. We would certainly stop them on the River Seine.

The first day the car had to wait for us. The second day the bicycles had to wait for the car. We were right in the midst of the refugees coming from Belgium, Northern France and Paris. We slept in a tent we had brought with us. During the day whilst the car was following the queue, Jack, Bob and I were going visiting farms to get something to eat. Practically all the farms had been abandoned and the cattle were left in the fields. More than once we had chicken or rabbit for lunch. We had no bread for over a week. The evacuees on the road were going very slowly. Our record was when one day the car started at 4 o'clock in the morning and stopped at 9 o'clock at night after covering 2½ kilometres (about 1½ miles). Everybody thought it would be better after the Loire. The bridges on the river Loire were holding us up. After a week of travelling we heard that the Germans were only 60 kms behind us. We didn't stop that night and for 48 hours we kept going, with no lights at night and strafed by enemy planes during the day.

We were not that far from the Loire. We would cross the bridge at Sully-sur-Loire in the morning and then it would be alright. I then decided that if we did not cross the Loire in the morning, I would leave the rest of the family and cycle down to Bordeaux and try and get a boat for England.

In the morning at 4 o'clock we heard the bridge at Sully being blown up by a bomb. I was a few miles in front of the car and, at the village 6 kms from Sully. All the traffic was diverted to the east towards Gien, 28 kms up the river Loire, where we were to cross it. The bridge at Sully was so badly damaged that only pedestrians could use it. I decided to wait for the car and was there for about two hours in a café at the corner of the road. I saw a local Mayor and three captains having a drink. The Mayor said "I've sent my driver with the car to cross the river at Gien. Meanwhile we will walk to the Château on the other side of Sully and have a good time." The family arrived in an army truck. The car had had a breakdown and had been left on the side of the road with most of our belongings. We carried on towards Gien hoping to get there before the Germans.

Unfortunately when we were in sight of the bridge, firing began. The Germans were just arriving at the bridge.

I made my way forward between the cars to see what was happening when I met a French soldier walking back with bullets in his chest, and soldiers firing from behind the cars, I realised it was serious and came back to the car; it was 6 pm. The soldiers told us there were only a few German parachutists and we could proceed forward as soon as they were wiped out, but the firing went on until dark. Nobody knew exactly what to do. No officers were to be seen. Most of them were probably having a good time further south.

Sometime around midnight I said goodbye to my family and told them I was going to try and cross the river. The firing had practically stopped. I went forward with my bicycle and mixed up with French soldiers, I picked up a French helmet and waited with them; they were going to try and cross the bridge. After a couple of hours waiting, we got up and walked towards the bridge. The night was quiet except for explosions coming from two burning trucks containing ammunition. When we passed these two trucks, a French NCO stopped all the civilians. Only men in uniform could pass, but with my helmet and raincoat I managed to pass with the soldiers. About 400 metres from the bridge we met a few men who told us the bridge was now guarded by Germans.

We went back towards the burning ammunition trucks where the same NCO stopped me and asked for my papers. I showed him my British passport and Identity card but he said I was a fifth columnist and that he was going to shoot me! I insisted I was British and had my correct papers but he said, "They all have." He then called a soldier and handed me over to him. The soldier put his revolver in my back and pushed me to the machine gun post. There, by sign language – he could not speak French – he told me to lie down next to the machine gun. Ten minutes later I was sound asleep; I had been cycling for 48 hours non-stop. Sometime later a French captain came along, had a look at my papers and told me I could go. I found my family along the road and we eventually went to sleep in a barn. When we woke up, the French this side of the river had surrendered.

We were on the German side and we soon saw our first German, who came along the road shouting. Then came a car with four tanned Germans who took one of the farm buildings as an observation post. A couple of hours later the French artillery south of the river started to shell it; this continued all afternoon.

We were scattered in the field next to the farm and it's a miracle that we were not hit. In the evening, the Germans ordered us to move out. We found a pram, and after throwing away most of what was left of our luggage, we walked a mile up the road to an empty house. I went back to the barn twice under shelling to get some of our things. When I looked back after the second time the barn was ablaze. We slept on mattresses in the garden of the house. Next morning we started to walk back to Paris (200 kms) but were pushed to the side of the road in a field to let the German troops pass. We stayed there four days living on food found in abandoned farm carts all along the road. During these four days it was decided that everybody who had room in their car would take those who had no car. But when the Germans told us we were free, all the cars left without taking the people promised a lift.

In the fields, there were hundreds of horses left behind by French troops. I caught three of them and got hold of a farm cart and, at 7pm, in pouring rain, we started on our way back to Paris. It took us a week to get there but it was better than walking. We had to leave one of our horses in a farm. It had received a wound in the shoulder which had become infected.

I will never forget the last 500 metres at Vaucresson. I arrived galloping and shouting in a small bread delivery cart drawn by one of the horses. We found our sister, Joan, who had come back from Brittany with my aunt and uncle Blicklé. They looked pretty grim.

The armistice had been signed. Half of France was occupied. After a month or so, on the 28th June at 2 o'clock in the afternoon, a car stopped at our gate and two Germans and a French policeman asked for Mr. Hicks. They arrested my father and wanted to arrest me but I explained in a few words of German that I had been in France 20 years and they decided to leave me, but I was to report every day to the *kommandantur*. My father was sent to Fresnes prison. At that time the Germans arrested about 700 British subjects in Paris and the suburbs. They were kept in cells at Fresnes Prison for two months before being sent to internment camps.

I started work with my two horses, transporting wine for the local grocer. The mayor of the village had other ideas and requisitioned my horses and the cart. So I started another business, a bicycle repair shop, which worked alright until I was myself arrested on 8th October. During those last two months of freedom, my two brothers and I did a little burglary practice. A lot of houses in the district were empty, the people being in unoccupied France. One day I saw the Germans marking on the gates the number of soldiers who were going to occupy the houses, so we decided to visit these houses before the Germans and pinch all the food and wines we could find. That's how I learned to pick locks, which was very useful to me three years later. I remember finding in a cellar about 20 bottles of Champagne and 30 bottles of Sauterne 1921 and one of 1912.

St. Denis

On 8th October as usual I went to the *Kommandantur* to report, a German truck was waiting for me and a few other British subjects. We were arrested and taken to the Versailles *Kommandantur* with about 200 other British subjects who had just been arrested. The Germans gave us a plate of soup and after another truck had joined us, we were driven to Paris and then to Fresnes prison. I knew that all the British interned at Fresnes had been transferred to St. Denis a week earlier so I mentioned to the officer in charge that we should be taken to that prison, but he said his orders were to send us to Fresnes. There we were told that there was no room for us so we were sent back to the *Kommandantur* in Paris on the place de l'Opera where we were kept for two hours. We were then driven to Cherche-Midi prison, but upon arrival we found out this was also full and they could not take us. Not knowing what to do with the prisoners, the Germans took us back to Versailles *Kommandantur* at mid-night. They woke up the officers and after a lot of discussion and telephone calls, we started again for yet another destination. We were taken to Versailles Women's prison but they would not accept us. Then we were taken to St. Pierre prison at Versailles, no room here either. The Germans told us to sleep on the concrete floor of the corridor. This was my first night in prison!

In the morning we were given lukewarm ersatz coffee in a greasy tin. At 7.30 we were moved again and driven to St. Denis where I found my father. St. Denis

Internment camp was the old St. Denis Barracks with barbed wire all around the grounds. I was sent to room 67 with 6 others. There were bunk beds with straw and one blanket per person. The German rations consisted of a cup of ersatz coffee in the morning, a bowl of soup for lunch and a fifth of a loaf of bread with a piece of margarine and jam or cheese for supper. We were allowed a weekly parcel from people outside. Every fortnight we were allowed a visit from relatives or friends. This visit consisted of putting about a hundred internees in a big hut on one side of a long table going from one end of the hut to the other end and the hundred visitors on the other side of the table. The visit lasted half an hour.

After a few days of idleness, I thought it would be a good idea to find a job. I started working with the B.I.R.C., (British Internees Recreation Committee). We started organising sports, concerts etc. My work consisted of drawing posters for the concerts and sports meetings, and also typing a lot of letters for the Committee. The first six months passed rather quickly.

At Christmas we were all very pleased to receive our first Red Cross parcels. It was marvellous. Christmas cakes, Christmas puddings etc. We had a lovely Christmas dinner with a few bottles of wine we had received in a parcel from someone outside. On New Year's Eve, after dinner, I went round the building to pay a visit to some friends. In Fred Payne's room I found about thirty people drinking champagne. Fred was in charge of the canteen and had managed to smuggle two or three dozen bottles of champagne. I joined in and had quite a lot to drink. Sometime after midnight I found myself alone talking to Tom Waltham; Fred was in bed unconscious, like the other two inhabitants of the room. All the visitors had gone. Seeing everybody asleep we opened the window and took another bottle from the shelf, which I drank with Tom. After that I decided to go home but it was quite impossible. I was stuck on my chair and quite incapable of getting up! I woke up the next morning in the same room.

Between Christmas and Easter we did not receive any Red Cross parcels; we later learnt that the Spanish had pinched them. About 20,000 Red Cross parcels were stolen whilst in transit through Spain.

Volunteers were asked to form a Camp Police. I volunteered and worked for a few weeks until I was thrown out for knocking out an internee who didn't want to queue up for his dinner like the rest. Then I worked for six months on the vegetable garden. It was a pleasant change to see green vegetables and to get to eat them, instead of looking at the barbed wire all around the camp. Although this camp was a British internees camp, half the internees could not speak a word of English or had never set foot in England in their lives. Some of them had names like Christosomou or Stephanopoulos. A lot of the internees were racketeers, like the one who was in charge of the canteen and who used to sell a tooth brush case for 9 francs, when it was only worth 1f 25cts. In the summer we had sports every day. Tennis on a court made by the internees. Athletics, soft ball with the Canadians and of course cricket. In winter, football and when the weather got really bad, ice skating and ice hockey on the now ice covered tennis court. The winter of 1941-42 was very cold. We were living in huts and for over a month we had a quarter of an inch of ice on the walls inside. On the whole, conditions were not that bad; we had our Red Cross parcels, so we did have food. During the winter that year the Germans asked for a volunteer to go and light the fires in the Censorship Office and sweep the rooms. I got the job and every morning, at half past seven, I used to go outside the barbed wires and light the fire. After some time I thought my position with the Germans could be used to help somebody to escape. I talked about it to Franck Pickersgill and decided to help him to escape. At the end of January, a young internee escaped. His mother lived in Paris; the Gestapo didn't even go to visit her, even though the Germans had warned us that if somebody escaped there would be reprisals on the family of the person who had escaped. That prompted me to escape with Franck Pickersgill.

Every Saturday, I took Franck with me to help me sweep the rooms. The Germans didn't work on Saturday afternoons. The sentries had gotten used to seeing Pick come with me. We waited until the officer working in the Censorship Office went on leave. We'd received an axe saw inside a loaf of bread in one of the parcels, I also had a key made for the room of the officer who was on leave.

The first Saturday, the German NCO sent a sentry with us so there was nothing doing. The next Saturday, without saying anything to my father and two brothers, who by now had been interned a few months before, we went to work as usual. The sentry at the gate stopped us and sent us to see the NCO on duty. I walked to him, said good afternoon and talked about the weather, then I told him we were going to work as usual. He didn't send a sentry with us. Once in the building all we had to do was to saw a thick iron bar at the window and we'd be free in the street.

First we swept the room then having nothing to do until dark, went upstairs to the officer's room which we opened with our key and spent the afternoon lying on his bed listening to his radio set. It was snowing outside and pretty cold. At 8pm, we went down to the office and I realised that there was no hope of sawing the bar before curfew. There were too many people in the street. We waited until midnight. Pick was watching at one of the windows whilst I started to saw one of the bars at the other window. Four solid hours I sawed this bar, which was about one and a half inches thick. We could hear the sentries walking, and French policemen talking outside only about fifty yards from the window. Twice during the night we thought the sentries were coming in the office. Once we heard a sentry scraping his feet on the grate outside the door; luckily he did not come in. At 8am we got out through the window, closing it behind us and putting the iron bar in place. I learned later that it took the Germans two months to find out about this.

We took the bus to Paris, where we met some friends and stayed in Paris all day Sunday. On Monday morning we took the train to Dax, south of Bordeaux, where we were introduced to a young student from Paris, who showed us the way to the demarcation line. We had to sleep in the fields Monday night, having no papers to go to a hotel. It was raining but not too cold, being in the south of France. On Tuesday we took a bus to the demarcation line. About 10kms from the line a French Gendarme got on the bus and started asking everybody for their identity cards – of course we had none. All I could think of was barbed wires, prison iron bars and Gestapo. I was sure we were going to be caught, so near to freedom. At that moment the Gendarme had his back to us, I got up followed by Pick and we just walked off the bus, calm as you like. The Gendarme didn't say a word. A hundred yards further on, we got back on the bus again. The driver stopped in the woods about a couple of miles from the frontier to let us off. We walked for quite a time but lost our way and had to ask a French peasant, who was very kind, to help us. We crossed the line. At last we were free. The Germans could not arrest us now that we were in Free France. A hundred yards after the line Pick fainted from exhaustion and emotion.

Once in unoccupied France we could not be arrested by the Germans anymore, but we could be by the French police because we were foreigners and had no papers.

We went to Périgueux where Pick had some friends. We were wonderfully well received by these people. We decided to go to report to the French police in order to get new British identity cards. The *Commissaire de Police* shook hands with us and his first words were:

"Messieurs, je vous félicite, mais maintenant il faut que je vous engueule." [Gentlemen, I congratulate you, but you have no papers and you've been travelling without a pass. You will have to go into Correctionnelle (Court) next Wednesday].

On Wednesday we went to this small court, thinking that we would only have to pay a few hundred francs. We had some fun watching other people being tried. The first two had stolen two yards of rubber tube from the railway company. Then there was a woman who had six children, although she wasn't married, and could not pay the rent because her "husband" as she called him, used to keep all the money. Then a gypsy who had stolen a pound of margarine and sold a few clothing coupons, was called. They called a name which belonged to a Spanish girl, but she had not turned up. Having omitted to renew her foreigner's identity card, one of the judges sentenced her to fifteen days in prison. Then our names were called; Whitmore Hicks and Franck Pickersgill, the charge of having omitted to renew our foreigner's identity cards and travelling without a pass. Well we thought that should be something like a month in prison, if the Spanish girl received a fortnight for not having her identity card.

The judge asked us why we had not got identity cards. We answered him that we had escaped from a camp in occupied France and therefore we could not ask for our papers before leaving the camp. The judge looked at us and said, "Well, that is a different matter." He nudged his fellow judge and after discussing our case for a few minutes said that we were not guilty and could go home. I nearly burst out laughing in the court – I was so pleased. We got our papers the next day, but we were not allowed to leave the village without permission from the police. We wrote to the American Embassy and got an allowance of 1,400 francs a month.

Pick managed to go to Lyon, and after a medical visit was given authorisation to be repatriated. His visa took a long time to obtain but he was finally repatriated through Spain and Portugal in September. After three and half months at Périgueux, I got permission to go to the Creuse department for hay making. I spent a month on a farm, up at 4 in the morning, working all day until sometimes 9 pm. I didn't get on too well with the farmers, so in order to leave the farm and stop working for them, I decided to break one of my fingers. I put my middle finger on my left hand on two stones and hit it with a third stone. It is much more difficult to try and break a finger than you think. The first time it didn't break, I had to hit a second time. When it was broken, I went to see the farmer and told him I had damaged my finger. An old wall had collapsed and my hand had been trapped underneath, he took my word for it and sent me to a doctor who x-rayed the finger to find it was now in a V shape. He put it back in place.

Not being able to work, I left the farm the next day and took the train for Lyon to see my cousin André. I arrived at Lyon to find my cousin's wife, Josette, alone. André was on holiday at Puycalvel (Lot). I spent most of my time that month of August 1942 at the swimming pool.

I had to go back to the Creuse to fetch my luggage and a new pass for Lyon. The first one was only for a fortnight. Whilst waiting for this new pass I was camping alone in a field; sometimes I didn't see a soul for the whole day. I remember realising at the end of the day that I had not spoken to a single person. I spent September in Lyon always at the swimming pool or cycling along the Rhône with friends. In October André left his job and we both went to live in Puycalvel on his wife's farm. It was a small farm, uninhabited for years. I joined the local football team but had to get a pass from the police every time I wanted to go to the club. We did not do much work on the farm as it was the beginning of winter. The first match of the season I scored a goal but a few minutes later I got kicked in the right knee. I could hardly walk.

In November the Germans invaded unoccupied France and the French fleet at Toulon was scuttled. Jean, André's younger brother, was at Toulon at the time on the *Mammeluck*. He arrived a few days later and stayed about six weeks with us. We had quite a pleasant time all together.

Once the Germans were occupying the whole of France I wasn't allowed to leave the village at all. My papers were taken away from me by the Gendarmes, so I immediately bought a French identity card, filled it in with a French name and went to the mayor's house. He was a local farmer and all his stamps were in the kitchen. I asked for him but his wife said he was away and asked me to wait for him. When she went out I pinched the stamp and put it quickly on my card. With this French card I could travel like a Frenchman.

I went to Lyon, where I knew a girl who was working with the Resistance Group "Liberation". She said she could help me to get back to England through Spain and Portugal. In February 1943, I was introduced to two young Frenchmen who were going to take me to the Spanish Border. Unfortunately this was a day before the Germans established a forbidden zone on the Spanish border – the place was swarming with Germans. Patrols were all over the place. We were arrested by a French Gendarme 15 kms from the border. He kept us a few hours and then released us telling us not to go any further because of the Germans. He told us that they would arrest us and send us to Germany; his parting words were to try again later on. I went back to Puycalvel for the night but next morning, as I was getting up, two Gendarmes knocked at the door and asked if they could see the Englishman. Anticipating they were going to arrest me, I informed them they were too late and that the Englishman had gone to Lyon the previous week. They said it was a shame the Englishman was not here as they wanted to tell him he was going to be repatriated through Switzerland. They asked how tall he was, if he was fair and how he was dressed. I informed them I was my cousin and they believed everything I told them. They left, but went to see some of the neighbours to see what they knew about me. An old lady told them she had seen me the previous day so they came back and said they were going to be frank and said they did not want the Englishman to come to any harm, but they knew he was around. André looked at me and said that he had been here but that the Englishman had gone into the town which was about 16 miles from the village. André realised that they had not recognised me as the Englishman. The poor Gendarmes said they would have to go away and make yet another report and asked me to fetch the Englishman to them as soon as possible. I said I would and left for good the same day.

I took the first train for Lyon where I started working for the "*Libération*" resistance Group. I was sent to Marseilles one day to deliver 4,000 propaganda papers. Anyone found with those papers would be shot by the Gestapo. Everything went according to plan until Marseilles station. Getting out of the station the police stopped me and asked what I had in my suitcase. Some clothes, I said. I was told to open the case; I told them that I had lost the key, but that the case belonged to the lady who was in front of me. If they would hold the case for a moment, I would get the lady and the key. I walked right on out of the station, catching the next train to Lyon.

In March I met a British Captain who had been parachuted in France to organise the *maquis*. I was introduced to Nicholas in the backroom of a grocers shop. I asked him if I could work with him or if he could help me get back to England. He asked London but the answer was, *"have nothing whatsoever to do with him"*. He gave me 5,000 francs and wished me good luck. Disgusted with his first refusal, I left Lyon and went to visit a friend in Haute Savoie.

ALPS

Although it was April when I went to the Plateau d'Amy (Haute Savoie) to see my friend Fischer, it was snowing and cold. I arrived at Le Fayet - St. Gervais station at 12 noon. There was a snow storm and one could not see ten yards in any direction. I met Fischer at the station and we took the bus together. It took us about an hour to do the ten miles uphill to the plateau. There were ten to twelve sanatoria on this plateau; the altitude was 3,000 feet. I had been told that there was a lovely view from this plateau but owing to clouds and snow, nothing could be seen. On the third day, when I woke up, I saw a lovely blue sky through my window. I got up and was amazed by the marvellous scenery. I could see the chain of Mt. Blanc from Chamonix to the Italian frontier. All these mountains covered with fresh snow, with the sun shining, made an indescribable picture. I spent a week there doing nothing but resting and going for short walks. I liked the place so much that

154

I decided to go and get my luggage at Lyon, where I had left it, and come back to live at the plateau. I got an apartment in a nice little chalet and could take my meals at any of my friends' sanatoria. One day a young doctor invited me to go with him climbing. So one morning at 5am we started for the plateau de Platé (7,000 feet) with our lunch, a good pair of boots and no experience. We climbed for four hours before we reached the snow. We met two young Frenchmen coming down. They warned us that there were *maquis* in a hut on the plateau. We reached the plateau about 10am and made for the hut half buried under the snow which was several feet deep on the plateau. We found the *maquis,* who were surprised to see us. After we explained what we were doing, they gave us a cup of coffee. After lunch, we decided to climb a bit further on towards the Aiguille de Platé. We climbed for two hours, the snow was still frozen and it was quite an easy climb. On our return to the hut we started sliding down sitting on our heels *"en ramasse"*. I went down first and stopped after two or three hundred yards. When the doctor tried he lost his balance and came down at a terrific speed, sliding on his back. When he arrived at the bottom of the slope he had no more seat in his trousers and his arms were bleeding. We finally reached the village at 8pm feeling very tired. I went for a walk the next day on my own. I met some boys at one of the chalets de Warens. They did not look like the *maquis* I had met the previous time.

When I got to my chalet I noticed that all the chalets were being guarded by Italian soldiers. I was immediately asked for my papers and arrested. I had my French papers with the name Georges Germain on them. I was told I would be taken to Sallanches where my ID card would be verified. I realised they had just arrested some of the *maquis* and thought I was one of them. I decided to escape at all costs.

We were allowed to walk about freely between the chalets, but could not go any further. On one side was a steep slope with clouds very low. I decided to rush down the slope. I was just going to start my run when I heard the voices of two Italians just around the corner of one of the chalets. One was an officer, the other his NCO. I asked if I could talk to him. I told him I was wet and, as my medical certificate stated, I had tuberculosis. I was in a sanatorium, and I would catch cold. I asked him to release me so I could go back to the sanitorium where, if he wanted, he could come and see me. He took my name and address and said he would see me in a couple of days time. He sent me away and I ran all the way back to the village in about 20 minutes. I never heard from these Italians again.

I was introduced to a girl, who was the daughter of a famous Chamonix guide. She asked me to join her and her friends to go with them to climb every weekend. Amongst her friends was Robert Delmas who used to spend all his spare time climbing. He knew all the mountains around the area. One night in August I was woken up at 1am by an explosion. I got up and saw a red glow coming from the valley. We could hear planes passing over head. The Cheddit factory had been bombed, said Fischer. Before I reached the point from where we could see the valley I heard another bomb whistling down. I threw myself on the ground and waited. Then the explosion came. It was 80 yards away from me. We later learnt that it was not the factory that had been bombed but a couple of small farms. There were loads of injured people, so I helped those I could, including a woman who was wounded in the arm and leg. I managed to find a doctor who looked after them. I went to bed at 4am and so the next days' climbing was cancelled.

My sister Joan came to see me at the end of July. We went haymaking for some of her stay. That is not as easy as it sounds when you are in the mountains. We also went on some long walks in the mountains. One was a very long walk and, to be honest, I do not know how she managed to do it. I went on climbing with various people and acted as a guide to some others. During the month of August, I took quite a few clients to climbs I knew very well. All I asked of them was that they fed me during the expedition.

The summer coming to an end, I decided to go back to Lyon and try and contact Capt. Nicholas and ask him again if I could join him. I arrived in Lyon on the 1st September. Before I left, I found two letters waiting for me, one was to announce that my grandmother had died and the other was informing me that my cousin André had died two days later.

RESISTANCE

I tried to contact Nicholas but learnt from Mr. Niel that he had gone back to England. He was nearly arrested by the Gestapo in March or April – he met the two Gestapo agents, who were going to arrest him, on the staircase. He jumped over the railing losing a shoe and his hat and ran away in the street. His radio operator, Marius, was also wanted by the Gestapo. He was in hiding and slept with a sten gun under his pillow. I had asked to meet Marius, but he would not see me for security reasons. He did, however, ask me for my particulars and asked London once more if I could work with them. Waiting for the answer, I joined France d'Abord and worked with Niel getting information about *milices* and Gestapo agents.

At the beginning of November, I was told to go and meet Henri at the café du Caveau. He told me that I was accepted by London and was to report to Marius, at the Gasworks in Cluny (Saône et Loire), about 100 miles north of Lyon. I met Marius at 10am the next morning. He was a dark man with a slight English accent. He told me I now belonged to the British Army and that if I worked well he would recommend me for a command. I was to work with Tiburce, another British Captain, who was dropped the previous week. He was to show me how to use a sten gun, other types of guns and explosives. I was asked if I wanted new French identity papers. I said mine were good enough. Tiburce had an accent of a mixture of Spanish, southern French and English. Apart from his slight accent, he spoke perfect French. We had various men from the village with us – Georges Malère, manager of the Gasworks, and Jean Renaud, an undertaker, had both been in the Resistance since the very beginning of the war. We had Lieutenant Guillaume, a young French officer from St. Cyr military school with us.

I met Jean Louis also, a young Frenchman, with clear blue eyes and very fair hair. He could probably kill anybody or derail a train or direct any attack on the Germans. In November, the Germans offered 200,000 francs for any information leading to the arrest of any terrorist. We found a letter at the post office addressed to the "Sicherheit Dienst Polizei" in other words Gestapo, saying that a young boy of 19, living in Cluny, had some information about terrorists. We gave the letter to Jean Louis. A couple of days later at 6pm a black Citröen stopped in front of the factory, where the boy was working. Two men asked for the boy, producing Gestapo papers. They took the boy into the car and drove off. The boy told them all he knew about the *maquis* of the neighbourhood, he gave the names of twenty young comrades, with whom he had been with for about 6 months before. Jean Louis was one of the Gestapo men and asked the boy if he knew anything about us. He said he didn't, but would find out and tell all he learnt. That was enough for Jean Louis who told the boy they were not the Gestapo but the Free French police, and that the boy was a traitor. The boy was executed at dawn the next day.

Sometime later, four Feld Gendarmes arrived at a village a few miles away from Cluny to arrest two Italians. The underground got wind of this and decided to shoot the Gendarmes. They killed one, but two ran away, one of whom was severely wounded in the chest. They took the fourth one prisoner. He was taken to a wood and shot. I was asked to go and help them bury the dead German. The next day a strong party of Germans arrived and set fire to a couple of houses and took hostages. Very soon the whole area was occupied by German troops.

A few of the German NCOs would stop and have their meals in the restaurant where I would eat. I used my German to make friendly talk with them. They told me they were looking for terrorists. One of them said to me that he thought I did not look like a Frenchman, more like a German. I told him that was probably because my grandmother was German. After that they thought they were my friends! They enjoyed their drinks and together with Georges Malère, Jean Renaud and Cugnet we were buying white wine for them all the morning. We had various toasts including one for my "boss" (Churchill), who was ill at that time. They lifted their glasses and drank, not knowing it, to Churchill's health.

One day I was sent by Tiburce to St. Gengon, to find out something about another of our *maquis* who had been attacked a few days earlier, by the Germans. I arrived at the station and went to the café opposite, in the hope of meeting a contact for the *maquis*. He wasn't there but I saw somebody else. He was Maltese and was employed by the railway company. I had spoken to him before. He told me he had been arrested by a Gestapo Captain and had been kept all night in a room. He suddenly looked up and said, "Here he is." I looked up and saw a civilian coming in followed by four Gestapo men in uniform armed with sten guns. They took up their positions at all the entrances of the café. The civilian (Gestapo Captain) came straight to me and asked for my papers. I handed over my wallet. He emptied it completely and asked me all sorts of questions for twenty minutes. Having answered all his questions with a smile, I was given back my wallet and told I could go. Needless to say, I didn't hang around.

I spent a week with Jean Louis travelling all over the area on the back of his motorbike. We went on reconnaissance once, to study the telephone lines along the main railway going through Châlons.

At the end of January 1944, the troops evacuated Cluny. I was to be sent to another region as an organiser. I went to the Ain *department* about 60kms east of Lyon. My targets would be the three main lines meeting at Amberieux, one of them being the main line to Italy, the other one to Switzerland and Germany. My job was to find as many men as possible who would go to the woods and mountains on D-Day to blow up railways and attack all German transports. The only contact I had in the district was one young farmer.

I had to organise reception committees, to enable us to receive supplies parachuted by the RAF, at night. I had been to two or three parachute drops with Tiburce around Cluny, but every time the plane had failed to arrive. Curfew was at 10 pm but we used to leave Cluny just before 10 in a lorry, armed with sten guns, and spend the night outside waiting for the plane.

Tiburce was a fine fellow. He was not parachuted into France but dropped in by a plane which landed and he walked off. Unfortunately the reception committee that was waiting for him was composed of the worst kind of criminals he had ever seen, according to his own words.

They gave him a bicycle with no brakes and when they had to go through a village, would make him go in front, as they thought there might be Germans there. He got to the station at last and took the train to Lyon. He felt very tired after his trip but would not go to sleep because when he woke up he had the habit of saying "*Good morning, everyone*". He may well have encountered Germans. He remembered that he had been given two types of pills, one to help him sleep for 24 hours and the other one to keep him awake, the only problem was he could not remember which was which. When he arrived at Lyon he went to the address that had been given to him by London only to find the woman who was there worked for the Germans. I really do not know how he was not arrested.

A lot of mistakes had been made to do with the parachuting in of supplies and people. I met one chap at Cluny who had just been parachuted in. He had been dropped on the wrong ground and was nearly shot by a reception committee, who thought he was a German. They were not expecting anyone to arrive that evening. This guy told me that he had been in training with Pickersgill and that he had been dropped into France three months earlier.

ON MY OWN – AIN

The young farmer was waiting for me at the station. He had been told that he would have a German magazine *Signal* in his right hand. Jean was a young man of 22, living on a farm with his old father, sister and brother. After an hour's walk we arrived at his farm in the mountains. He had formed, with his brother, a small group of six would-be *maquis*. I gave my first lesson on how to use a sten gun and an automatic pistol, and more importantly how to clean them. I soon found out that only Jean and his brother François would be any good. The others liked to talk about fighting and shooting but when it came to action they were not that enthusiastic about it.

We had been told to expect a drop by parachute. A message would be transmitted by the BBC, the message was *Le chou à la créme est le meilleur* (creamed cabbage is the best). One night in February we heard this message. As it had been snowing, three of the group refused to go. François, Jean and the youngest of the group volunteered to come with me to the top of the mountain and wait for the plane. After walking for two hours in deep soft snow we reached the plateau. The snow was waist-deep in parts and with a strong cold north wind blowing, our clothes were wet and frozen by the wind. We lit a fire under a tree to try and get warm. About three hours later we heard a plane going around. We rushed to our respective spots and with three red torches and one ordinary torch, we sent the letter C in code. Unfortunately, the mist was too thick for the pilot to see our signal, he tried a few more times to see the signal but with no luck. At 3 in the morning we started our journey back down the mountain, cold, very tired and disappointed. The walk downhill was just as difficult as the one going up. We arrived back at the village exhausted but satisfied we had tried our best. Later we got orders to blow up as many train engines as possible. Jean's uncle, who lived in Ambérieux, was an engine driver. Ambérieux was a big *"gare de triage"* or Marshalling Yard. Jean's uncle met me and took me inside the station to prepare to attack the engine depôt. Unfortunately we were stopped by a Vichy policeman who wanted to know what we were doing in the depôt. We said we did not know it was forbidden to visit the station and went on our way. The following evening, six engines were blown up. Somebody else had done the job. I kept travelling between Lyon and the village in the mountains. I went to Lyon twice a week to see Tiburce.

We only had one radio operator and we used to meet him in Lyon. On every journey the Germans would ask for our papers. On one occasion I was travelling with our radio operator, Maurice, when this dumb Feld Gendarme asked for our papers and if we had any weapons. We burst out laughing and said of course we had but not with us, and that they were back at home on the farm! He laughed and thought we were joking.

The Germans were having lots of trouble with the *maquis* in Savoie. A big offensive was launched by French police, Vichy *milice* and German SS troops against the *maquis* in February.

One evening I arrived at Terray station to find myself, along with all the other passengers, arrested by German Feld Gendarmes. We were kept in the station all night. Knowing a little German, I acted as interpreter for the other passengers. I asked one of the Germans for a pack of cards. He said he had some at his hotel but he could not leave us to go and get them. I insisted I wanted the cards and ordered him to go and get them. He came back with them and we had a game of *belotte* until three in the morning. At 7 we were taken to see the Kommandant, who was not very happy to see us as he was shaving. He told the sentries to take us back to the station. We assumed we were free to go about our business, so I caught the first train back to Lyon.

I met up with an old friend of France d'Abord. I asked if he knew anybody in my district who could help to organise another group. He sent me to Jean Dargaud at Pont d'Ain. My friend said to tell Jean that he had sent me. I introduced myself as a friend of Templar. Jean Dargaud knew him quite well. I informed him I was British and I wanted to form a new group in Pont d'Ain. Dargaud started to act strangely; he had not heard from Templar for some time and thought I was a Gestapo agent. He was ready to take me down to the cellar to have a drink and then shoot me. Luckily for me he decided to wait and make sure of my identity.

I found out that some Feld Gendarmerie had gone to the farm in the mountains, asking about me. They had been told I lived there and were going to arrest me. I decided to keep away from the farm and concentrate on the Pont d'Ain group. Many a time we got messages to be ready to receive a drop, only to wait in vain. I tried to form a group at Ambérieux, with the help of the assistant station master but a lot of people had recently been arrested. Those who were not, were not prepared to take any more risks.

Through a friend in Lyon, I was introduced to Philippe, head of the F.U.J. at Bourg. F.U.J. was a minor French organisation, principally composed of young students. Philippe agreed to attack my targets, if I could arrange for a drop for him. He had about three hundred men in and around Bourg. With his help I formed another group at St. Rambert, to replace the small group at Jean's farm.

By the middle of March I had an assembled group at Pont d'Ain of about 30 men, a group at St. Rambert with 50 men, a group at Bourg with Philippe, and a small *maquis* of ten with Bouboule, a young Pole, as chief who was supposed to come from another district, on the other side of the Rhône and take the Lyon-Ambérieux line as their target.

At the end of March Tiburce had a new lieutenant. He decided to send him to me so that he could help me and take charge of the area as soon as possible. About this time I was introduced to a young Canadian Captain called Jean Paul – he had a terrible Canadian accent. He did not know what a *sou* was, although this was not surprising really as the currency *sou* had been abolished in 1793. He knew about francs and centimes however. After taking him to Pont d'Ain we got our message on the radio but as usual the plane didn't come. We went onto St. Rambert and walked up the mountain to see a new parachute ground; Jean Paul was out of shape and was sweating and cursing all the way.

We had a drop a few days later. The plane started to come in and we saw the parachutes coming down but they were not open. One had a container which, when it hit the ground, exploded because it had grenade detonators in it. We counted the parachutes; there were 18 but no men. This must be a mistake we thought, we heard another plane coming over head and thought this must be the one carrying the two men we were expecting, but no, another 18 parachutes came down with more gear. Now we only had a small car with us so how were we to get them back to base? We had a girl with us who was the girlfriend of the chef of a *maquis* unit in the district. We told her to wake him up and bring a truck with as many men as possible. She returned with her boyfriend, twenty men and a five ton truck. When we got to their camp, we opened the containers and shared everything.

Many railway lines were blown up more often now. One night the Germans were mending the line near St. Rambert when one of our planes came over. The pilot saw the German light and probably thought it was the reception committee he was looking for. It passed over the lights very low and the Germans opened fire with their machine guns. The plane was shot down and fell 4 or 5 miles further on near the Pont d'Ain. The crew were killed and burnt except for two men who had time to jump. A third one had jumped but had fallen on a pole and was killed. The two airmen who jumped were hidden in the mountains by the *maquis*.

We would meet at Julien's office once a week, it was on one of these occasions that I was informed by my English chief Tiburce, that I had become a member of the British Army S.O.E. Special Forces and was promoted to Sub-Lieutenant. I was given my service number, but I had no formal papers.

D-Day

On the first of June we received a message telling us that D-day would be between the first and fifteenth of June, and we would therefore have to attack our targets 48 hours after hearing another message warning us of D-day.

Since the first of June, Jean Paul and I, helped by two or three men, were looking for a suitable place in the mountain for our camp. We found a group of barns, only used in the summer for the hay-making seasons and decided to use a couple of them. We would need flour to make bread for the men. The miller of a village in the mountain had two tons of flour and was quite willing to sell it to us, but the Food Ministry decided to come and fetch it on the 6th June. The miller warned us two days before so we decided to attack the truck loaded with flour and requisitioned it for our use. On 5th June we got our second message. This meant that D-day would be on the 6th or 7th June and we were to attack all railways on the 7th June.

We got up at 5 am and about seven of us armed with sten-guns waited for the truck on the road. At 8 am we heard the truck coming down the hill. Two men jumped out of the bushes where we were hiding and stopped the lorry. The driver was scared. The miller was sitting next to him but didn't say much. We were not supposed to know him. We told them that we were going to take the flour and pay for it. On our way we saw a small truck belonging to a coalman from Lyon who had come to fetch some wood. We thought it would be useful to have a second truck so we just took it and I signed a chit for the driver saying that I had requisitioned his vehicle for the *maquis*. Before we took the truck, I sent someone to the Mayor of the village to tell him not to phone the police and not to tell anybody what he was going to see. We told him the Allies were going to land very soon, so he had better keep quiet. He replied that the Allies had already landed. This was how we learned that the invasion had begun. Everybody in the village was at their doors waving to us with broad smiles.

We sent one ton of flour to our group at Pont d'Ain and kept the other one for ourselves. We had to requisition food supplies, as we had new arrivals joining us all that day and the next; men coming to join the *maquis*. On the 7th June we selected 10 men to do the first sabotage on the railway line. We got the charges ready during the afternoon. We left at 11pm in the lorry and stopped about a mile from the railway line. We placed a few sentries and walked quickly towards the railway. When we got there, Jean Paul and I took the charges whilst three men armed with sten guns went to see if there was anybody on the line. Unfortunately there was a German patrol on the line. Two of the group opened fire, killing two and wounded two or three others. We started to run away, but after about 50 yards I thought this was silly so I stopped and had a look to see if the Germans were following us. The Germans had started shooting in all directions. They threw a few hand grenades and left with their dead and wounded. I walked back to the lorry to find one of our men wounded in the shoulder by one of our sentries. To complete the unsuccessful night the lorry wouldn't start and we had to walk back to the first village where we borrowed a horse and cart. We got back to camp at 6 in the morning. After this we realised that everybody needed training.

We had many more areas to go to. We met up with other *maquis* groups and helped train them in handling guns and explosives. At one place we learnt that the Germans were attacking in the Valronney. The Captain of one of the groups wanted to take positions at the Col.

Des Sapins. It was only for the night, to cover the retreat of other groups.

Tiburce came to visit one day when I was away, but Jean Paul was there. Tiburce told Jean Paul that they had quite a few battles in Saône et Loire. Jean Louis had been wounded by fifteen pieces of shrapnel in his back. Poor Jean Louis, this was the second time he had been wounded. The first time he'd been wounded was in February, when he was going to pinch some petrol during the night with a small truck. Unfortunately he was stopped by a party of Germans who were burning a house. He ran away but got four sten gun bullets through his body. He was found by our people the next morning in a barn, nearly dead, and taken to hospital.

Tiburce had found six unexploded 500 kilo bombs, dropped in the fields by the R.A.F. He thought of using four of them to destroy a big concrete bridge on the main line. They put four bombs on an old truck and placed plastic all round the bombs. They drove the truck under the bridge, lit the fuses and ran away. The bridge was blown up and the line cut for a few days. My targets were attacked regularly. The Ambérieux-Culoz line, the main line to Italy, was completely blocked after a week and remained blocked all the time. I decided to make a big attack on La Tour-du-Pin station to blow up all the "Cours d'Aiguilles" and all the engines. For this I was going to take twenty men on my lorry and eighty of Jules' men, on four of their trucks. The attack was going to take place on Saturday 4th August. On the third I had to go and visit Jean Dargaud's group near Pont d'Ain. Jean had been wounded and was coming back from hospital on that day. I had fresh orders to give to him. To reach their camp, which was about 25 kms from ours, I had to cross flat country infested with Germans, police etc . . . The best way of going there was, of course, in civilian clothes and without weapons.

On 3rd August I put my civilian clothes on and with my horse and cart and a young farmer, left the camp. We went through St. Rambert, Ambérieux and then took the small roads to a place on the road to Bourg where I was to meet Jean at noon. I waited there until 3 pm but nobody came. I had an idea of where Jean's camp was but I didn't know exactly. We drove to the wood where I thought I'd find the camp, but on the road we met Jean's sister, Jeanette, who was with André, an ex-station master who was now working for us. Jean was still in hospital and hadn't been able to come. We visited the camp and had a good tea. I didn't want to give the orders directly to the men. I wanted Jean to be the only one to know them. Jeanette asked me to go to their house in Pont d'Ain. The Vichy Militia had been occupying the village until the morning but were now replaced by Gendarmes and they wouldn't do anything, so we felt fairly safe. Thinking I could give Jeanette all the instructions for her brother, I accepted her offer of going to her house. We left the camp on bicycles. André was a hundred yards in front of Jeanette, and I was about the same distance behind. Going through Varambon I noticed a few people on their door step looking towards Pont d'Ain but I didn't pay any attention. A few hundred yards further on I passed three civilians walking on the road and just after a turning, I found myself in front of half a dozen *milices* armed with sten guns and a Bren gun on the roof of a car. I looked around and realised that the three civilians whom I had passed were the *milices* who had just arrested a young Frenchman. It was too late to go back so I decided to try my luck with my identity papers as I had done this before many times.

When I showed my papers the *milice* looked satisfied and was going to give them back to me when another *milice* came along and searched me, taking everything out of my pockets. Finding nothing important, he had a look at my papers and decided he would arrest me to verify my identity. I was taken away with three armed *milices* in the car and three others on the roof of the car. We arrived at the *milice* H.Q. at Bourg, where we were given dinner, but of course I couldn't eat. After the meal, the Frenchman and I were taken to a small room on the fifth floor. Half an hour later the Frenchman was taken away and I remained alone in my small room. Looking at the window I saw a ridge about a foot wide going along the wall outside. I could walk on the ridge and get to the corner of the house. But I would have to find out what was on the side of the building. There seemed to be a space about 9 feet wide between my building and the next house. I slept during the night and the next morning I was taken to a room where I was interrogated by a fat *milice*. They had rung up the Prefecture de la Drôme where my identity card was supposed to have been made and of course they found out that it was not on the records. Therefore it was a false card. I agreed that it was a false card but I maintained that my name was Georges Germain. I had altered the age in order to avoid being sent to Germany. They didn't believe it but they didn't get anything else out of me that time.

In the afternoon from the window in the corridor, I saw the building opposite. I thought it would be possible to jump from the ridge onto the roof of the next house and from there probably climb down to the street. Unfortunately, later on I was seen leaning out of my window to study the possibility of escaping so an armed sentry was placed in the street with orders to shoot me if I was seen at the window.

In another interrogation I had a pistol pointing at my back and threatened with torture if I didn't tell the truth. I told them a long story. From the short report in English, given to me by Jean Paul, I learnt they had found out that I had something to do with the *maquis* and believed I was an *"agent de liaison"*. I therefore built a story round this. I said I had accepted to do this job for money. Hoping they might ask me to work for them for more money. I also told them that before doing this I was a black marketeer. All that, to try and make them believe I was interested in money.

The next day I was interviewed by the Commandant, who was called Simon. He gave me his word of honour he would not hand me over to the Gestapo. He also said he was anti German. He was only doing his duty; maintaining order. And when the Allies arrived he hoped to be doing the same thing for them. In the afternoon the Commandant called me and said I was going to be interrogated by three men of the French police.

I was sent to a room and interrogated by these three men, they showed me their French police identity cards saying they had nothing to do with the militia. They also hated the Germans. One of them began by saying my name wasn't Germain but Moser. I was very surprised because I had a card with the name Moser but it was in the *maquis,* and only half a dozen people knew I had it. This card was registered at the Mairie, so there was no harm in admitting my name was Moser but when they asked me my date of birth and place of birth, I could not remember so I had to tell them it was another false card.

After that they told me I had been arrested by the Feld Gendarmerie, at Tenay in February; that I was a British officer and was working with the Canadian Group, at St. Rambert. In other words they had found somebody who knew me and had told them who I was. The only thing they didn't know was my real name.

I decided to tell them my name, and try another method altogether. I played the game of a British officer, placing honour first and that I was not interested in politics but only in military operations. I was sent back to my room. After dinner half a dozen young *milices* came into my room with a rope. They tied my feet together and my hands behind my back, and the rest of the rope around my neck. Then they started hitting me with their fists and kicking me. They cut my lips, I was bleeding all over my shirt. They left me bleeding, bruised and all tied up on my bed. I decided I would escape during the night with the help of the rope. I could easily undo it. About an hour later the commandant came in with two or three of his lieutenants. He had heard what had happened and said he was very sorry about it. They cut the rope and apologized. Simon said he had told the *milices* off and had sent one of the men to another unit. Unfortunately they took the rope away and put a projector in the street, lighting my window. The next morning I was called again by the Commandant. I was alone in his office. He said once again he had no intention of handing me over to the Germans. He wanted me to help him to stop the *maquis* from killing all the *milices*. He asked if I could do it. Of course, I could do that, I told him. We discussed the ways of doing this. The next morning he called me again, handcuffed me and said he was taking me to Lyon to see his superior officers about what we were going to do. He couldn't act without their consent. We travelled safely to Lyon in his car with a young *milice* on the roof with a Bren gun. I was hoping somebody would attack the car but nothing happened. I got out of the car in front of the *milice* H.Q., which was the newspaper *Le Progrès* building. Simon asked me not to attract the people's attention, but I was pleased to do as much as I could, with my five day old beard, cut lips, bloody shirt and being handcuffed. I waited nearly an hour whilst the Commandant was talking with his superior officer, Paul Touron.

When he came out he looked a bit embarrassed and said I was to be taken by two young *milices*. One had a riding whip and the other one a powerful lamp or torch. I immediately thought they were going to take me down to a cellar and beat me. They took me to a car and I was driven to a school, which was used as a prison by the *milice*. I was given lunch. All the *milices* were very proud of having what they thought was a British parachutist. One of them tried to tell me a lot of things in broken English, I let him talk for some time then told him in French that I could speak French as well, if he wanted me to. He was rather vexed. I was sent to a big room already occupied by two *milices,* who were there for disciplinary reasons. We had a wireless set and a good bed. One of the *milices* was an ex-army officer who had joined the *milices* and had refused taking orders from other *milices* who were not officers in the French army. The other one was an Arab. He had joined the militia for the money he was offered and didn't think he was doing anything wrong working for them.

Two or three hours later I was taken away in a car by the Commissaire Regional of the *milice*. I did not know where I was going. We turned on the Place Belcour and entered a court yard. When I got out of the car I saw two German sentries at the gate and at the entrance was written: Sicherheit-Dieutz-Polizei; that meant the Gestapo. I was simply handed over to the Gestapo with an accompanying report about me. I can't explain what I felt when I realised where I was. I was taken over by a short Gestapo man who asked me a few questions and ordered me to write on a piece of paper: *Je suis arrêté pour faux papiers* (I was arrested for false papers), and sign it W. G. Hicks. This was to be sent to Jean-Paul. I was then sent down to a cellar. As I went down the corridor, I noticed three rooms full of men and women sitting on chairs and benches, facing the wall in silence. In the corridor were two sentries with guns. I sat on a chair and waited in silence like everybody else. Time doesn't pass quickly in these conditions. A red-haired girl was sitting next to me. I noticed she was attractive. She whispered a few words to me. But we couldn't say much. The sentry was watching, it was the second time she had been arrested. At 10 o'clock they closed the door and we were allowed to talk and sleep on the concrete floor, if we wanted to. We were about a dozen people in the room. There were no windows and there was a kind of damp heat, and stuffy atmosphere. There was a young couple, about thirty years old, from Valence. They had been helping the *maquis* by providing identity cards from the prefecture. My own was probably one of them. There was also an old couple, about sixty, two or three Jews, an Austrian Jew and two young *maquis*. The girl with the red hair was called Ginette Estève. She used to work with my cousin André and his wife, and had heard of the English cousin when I was at Lyon, in 1942. I was told an American major, a parachutist, was being interrogated by the Gestapo. My morale was pretty low that evening. I didn't sleep that night but I talked with Ginette. She managed to get my morale up and in the morning I was feeling much better. We waited all the morning. From time to time the Germans called a name for interrogation. The prisoner used to come back two or three hours later with blood all over their face, broken arms or legs and sometimes on a stretcher. The P.P.F., Doriot's party were working with the Gestapo on the top floor of the building. The torturers/interrogators were led by Francis, an awful looking thug – broken nose, distorted mouth etc.

In the afternoon my turn came. I was taken upstairs, I was to be interrogated by R. Bahr, a Gestapo officer. He could not speak French and had to use an interpreter. I was interrogated for four hours. I answered all their questions and told them everything I was sure they knew already. At one moment they wanted to know names and addresses of resistance people living in Lyon. I said

I didn't know any. They didn't believe me and gave me a beating. They then said that if I didn't talk they would change their method. I was told to stand in the corner of the room facing the wall. The interpreter went out and came back a quarter of an hour later. I thought they were going to start their usual tortures. When the interpreter came back the interrogator went out and the interpreter told me to sit down and started to talk to me nicely. After talking for some time he told me he was commanding at Gien when they took the place in 1940. I told him we were there too. Then we talked about the difference between the German race and the British. He said that when he looked at me he could not help thinking about the young Germans of my age. He said I could easily be mistaken for a German. I asked him what he thought of the war. This was around the 10th August and the Allies were advancing in Normandy. He said he was sure the Germans and the Allies were going to come to an agreement and turn against the Russians; I, of course, agreed. When the interrogator came back we carried on very quietly. They didn't insist about the resistance people in Lyon.

I was sent back to my cellar. There I met C. Mauniere, the American major who had been brought from Montluc prison for interrogation. My first sign to him was a thumbs-up. Later on we managed to sit next to each other and whisper a few words. He had been dropped in by the *maquis* but when he was caught in civilian clothes by the militia, he had his uniform in a rucksack and put it on. He told me there was also an American parachutist lieutenant at Montluc. In the cellar now we had a few Polish officers who had been working underground. The wife of a Polish major had been arrested and she'd gone mad. I was interrogated every day and sometimes twice a day for four days with nothing to eat. One evening they brought down a man on a stretcher. He'd been tortured and beaten so much that he was unconscious. He was dead the next morning.

One of their tortures consisted of tying feet and hands together and passing a stick behind your knees and placing each end of the stick on either side of a bath tub full of very hot water. The head being heavier it went down under the water and one could not do anything about it. When you were nearly suffocated they would turn you around, so that you could breathe a bit, and then dip you again in the water. When nearly dead they'd take you out and beat you with sticks, bicycle chains etc, to warm you up. Another method was to put one's feet in boiling water or pull out your nails with pincers. One young couple, probably the couple from Valence, were being interrogated. They beat the husband, then the wife in front of the husband. This bringing no result, they then raped the wife in front of the husband; afterwards they put his feet in the boiling water. They were sent to Montluc prison. The man went to the infirmary where he was treated by the German Colonel in charge, who gave him cold foot baths every morning. After a few days he saw maggots on his legs. He told the doctor who said it was normal. Two days later he died. Everybody in the prison heard him screaming during his last night. After four days my interrogator came to see me with my report to sign. The report was in German. R. Bahr guaranteed that it was everything I had said. I signed it. This report was going to be sent to the big chief of the Gestapo, who would decide on my case. There was no doubt that I would be shot! After that I was sent to Montluc prison.

I was thrown into cell 113 which was only seven feet by six and already occupied by six other prisoners. The place was filthy. A small window at the top facing south. This cell was just like an oven. Amongst the other prisoners were Doctor de Botton, who'd been working with the resistance in the information section, a young boy of 19 or 20, Michel Triquet, who had been caught when he was going to join the *maquis*, and an old man of 75 from Montélimar who had been arrested with his son, and didn't know why. There was also Pierre Georget, a tall boy of 27. He had been arrested because he was using Gestapo papers to extract money from Black Marketeers. He was a real bandit. He had been in jail three or four times before for theft. At one time during the occupation he had eleven million francs. He promised me a million francs if he'd get out alive. We could just manage to sit down but we couldn't all lie down at the same time. The place was full of bed bugs and lice. We couldn't sleep before three o'clock in the morning because of the heat and the bugs. I was bitten all over and thought I was going mad with the scratching. At six in the morning the Germans used to wake us up with a cup of lukewarm ersatz coffee. At ten we had a piece of black bread with a teaspoon of butter to share between seven of us. At 12.30 we were given a pint of liquid (and very hot) vegetable soup – this had to be eaten with a wooden spoon and in five minutes, otherwise they would take away your tin if you hadn't finished it. The result was we had to eat quickly, burn our tongues and then sweat for a quarter of an hour afterwards. During the day we were all naked, it was much too hot to wear anything; we only had a drop of water at six o'clock. In the mornings we would be taken out into the Courtyard to wash in groups of 20, we had five minutes only. We would be marched in columns and were not allowed to talk. If we did talk or did not walk fast enough, we would be kicked or beaten. Time dragged slowly. To keep our minds active, Dr. de Botton would give us lectures in the afternoon. One evening we told each other any joke we could remember; needless to say we laughed all night. No one in our cell had a watch but someone in the next cell had one and by knocking on the wall, we had a code enabling us to ask for the time and pass it onto the next cell, if they wanted it. We even managed to communicate with one of the women's cells on the ground floor, through a pipe in the wall. This was the worst time of my life. One evening they brought in an old man I'd seen in Lyon. He used to work with Jules and had been arrested before. The Gestapo had poured boiling water over his head! He told me that André, the Canadian wireless operator, was still there in the prison. The old man from Montélimar was freed one day without having been interrogated – he had been there for one month and did not know why.

On 19th August we learned that the allies had landed in the South and we were hoping they'd come quickly. In the evening after eight o'clock, the Germans started calling out names and opening doors, probably taking out prisoners. At that time of the day it was not for interrogation. We knew that when they were going to shoot people: it was either at four or five in the morning or in the evening. They opened our door and called a name. It was the old man who was a friend of Jules. We were only four in the cell by then. The next morning at half past four they started again calling names. They came to our cell, opened the door and called two names; de Botton and Georget. They said good-bye knowing it was the end. Half an hour later they came back with the old man who'd been taken the previous day. We couldn't understand it. The old man told us there were about thirty or forty who spent the night in the cellar. They all thought they were going to be shot in the morning. He had seen André the Canadian and also an Englishman who had been a prisoner for some time. The other two had been sent downstairs where they were lined up in a corridor. There were altogether about eighty people, and they also thought they were going to be shot. The doctor told me once he knew he was going to die which was not so bad. The worst thing is to wait in your cell not knowing if you are going to be shot or if you are going to live. We had our coffee and half an hour later the Germans opened the door and called the three names again. This was the last I'd see of them. We were only two left in the cell. Michel and I. The next day the Germans collected all their belongings to give to the Red Cross. This meant they had been shot.

We were waiting our turn. Every time we heard footsteps in the corridor we followed the sound of them to know where they were going. Was it somebody coming to fetch us? We grew anxious if it came too near to our cell and relieved when it didn't stop in front of our cell. Through the window we saw a few Gestapo men counting Jews, we assumed they were taking them away to be loaded onto trains for Germany.

On 25th August we heard a lot of explosions in Lyon and two or three times Bren guns firing, and rifle shots in the town. In the evening at seven o'clock a sentry opened the door and asked for the British officer. I stood up and said goodbye to Michel. Downstairs the Commandant was waiting for me. The two Americans were there, handcuffed. The Commandant apologized for having to handcuff me and said he was taking me to Germany. "There is going to be joy in the prison tonight," he said, "we are evacuating the prison and everybody will be free". I was glad for all the prisoners and I thought that we would not reach Germany – soon we would be overrun by the Allies or else the *maquis* would stop us and there was a chance of escaping. I left the prison full of hope.

Unfortunately, it was only hope. I was taken, handcuffed, to Brunswick, to the British Officers camp, where I was warmly welcomed by the prisoners and put in isolation for some days until, I suppose, the

Germans found themselves satisfied with my story. Although Germany was slowly retreating and losing the war, I remained in the camp until April 1945; no ill-treatment, nothing much to eat and cold weather. During that time I had lost complete contact with my family. The last news I had received was that my father and two brothers were still in the camp at St. Denis. My mother and sister were in the camp at Vittel; they were taken there in 1943. Of course my parents had no news at all concerning my whereabouts and quite naturally they were very worried.

As soon as the Brunswick camp was liberated I tried to reach my uncle, Lord Alliston, who lived in Chislehurst in Kent, thinking that he and his wife, who was my mother's sister, would have news of my family and whether they were all alive or not. I received a reply to say that they were liberated at the end of October 1944, repatriated to the UK and all alive. They were also relieved and overjoyed to have news of me.

It was April, so I sent a message saying, "I hope to be with you all for Joan's birthday". I had no idea what had happened to them all. The last time I saw my little sister, she was just 13, now she was a young lady of 17, nearly 18, and was a junior clerk in an Insurance Company in London.

NOTE FROM JOAN HICKS: On St. George's Day, 23rd April, 1945, my 18th birthday, I was called down to the front hall of the company I worked for. There was my brother, dressed as a British officer, looking very thin but beautiful and looking at me as if he was seeing something most surprising! We threw ourselves into each other's arms, cried and spoke to each other in English, whereas up to the time we were separated in France, we always spoke French. I will always remember my 18th birthday. It was for us the end of the war.

Operation Manna

Kenneth E. Davey

The last year or so of the War was particularly hard on the Dutch, with food being severely scarce. This account features one of the R.A.F.'s humanitarian missions to alleviate Dutch hunger and drop food with the use of the wonderful Lancaster Bomber.

On 26th April, 1945, nobody knew that the war was to end 15 days later. R.A.F. Squadron 186, based at Stradishall near Cambridge, was given the task of dropping food to the Dutch, who were dying of hunger. The Germans must have been aware that the end was near and had, through the Red Cross, agreed to allow planes to drop food in a window of one hour on 28th April.

The Air Ministry had calculated that 350 Lancasters could participate, which meant they would pass at the rate of six per minute – weather permitting! We discussed at length the best way to go about it – drop from what height; how to pack the goods – spam, corned beef, potatoes, flour, dried vegetables etc. There was, of course, no question of parachutes and we didn't even have enough bags to put the stuff in.

On 27th April we carried out tests with 25kg bags dropped from 1000 feet. The sacks burst, the potatoes arrived mashed, the flour bags exploded like smoke bombs and the tougher items were distributed all over the landscape. Subsequent tests at 900, 800 then 600 feet made little difference. At 500 feet, however, which for a Lancaster was skimming the treetops, the potatoes landed unmashed. If we put them in two sacks, one inside the other, only the interior sack burst. The problem was partly solved by the armourers who adapted incendiary bomb containers which could carry 1250lbs of supplies in the bomb bays but much more could be carried if sacks were also loaded into the fuselage to be heaved out of the door by the crew members. Where on Earth, however, could we get thousands of sacks at 24 hours' notice? After some thought the Group Captain pointed out that the only place likely to be oversupplied in sacks, as for so much else, was likely to be the nearby US base.

An approach was duly made and the US Colonel was sympathetic and admitted to having in fact, vast quantities of sacks which he would be delighted to hand over – as soon as he had authority. Such an unusual request would probably have to go to the Pentagon, in an infinite series of small steps before being agreed to and the chances of getting it in 24 hours – zero. There was a silence, then, "Of course", the Colonel added, "Petty theft is a big problem and there aren't enough MPs to guard everything. Especially when the hangar isn't locked and the MPs are all on the other side of the base as they will be this evening. I don't suppose anything would be noticed until at least 20 minutes after the last sack left."

A nod is as good as a wink, hands were shaken and there followed a very busy evening. 1,500 heavy sandbags went unexpectedly missing that night. The local police were around at our base the next morning. The Chief Inspector went through the motions. "Americans seem to have lost a few bags. Don't suppose you chaps know anything about it? No? Well, I'll just note that for the record." He closed his notebook and was taken off for a gin and tonic in the Officers' Mess.

The mission, originally planned for the next day, was delayed for 24 hours by the Germans which gave us a little extra time to do the packing. The flight to Rotterdam was made at 1,000 feet, the ceiling being lower than forecast. Ten minutes from the city we had to come down even lower and we found ourselves surrounded by dozens of planes, all headed towards the same objective. In the crowd some delicate adjustments to motors 1 and 4 had to be made and the Rolls Royce Merlins didn't like being messed about with and not a few props had to be feathered. Later, back at Stradishall, the mechanics were most put out at the treatment we had been giving them. They had to work all night to get them back into operation for the next day. Some of the pilots weren't very happy either – several planes came back with bullet holes in them in spite of the promised cease-fire. They were only bullet holes though, there was no "ack-ack".

The scene on Rotterdam racecourse, the designated dropping zone, was extraordinary. Hundreds of planes were packed into the approach and you could see people scurrying about grabbing supplies while more was still dropping – this in spite of strict instructions to the contrary by the Dutch police. We learned later that several of these queue-jumpers were killed by falling sacks.

After the drop we flew over the city at 300 feet where the four-storey buildings and flat roofs were covered with orange flags and thousands of cheering people. Infected with their obvious enthusiasm we dropped to 200 feet along the wide avenues and really gave them something to look at.

There were another three or four operations of a like nature between then and the end of the war, at Rotterdam again, and also The Hague. Although what we could do was obviously very little in the face of so much need, the Dutch were very grateful. I left the RAF in 1962, after 20 years service, and settled in Paris. In 1970, I was invited to London, with other RAF officers who had participated in Operation Manna, by the Dutch ambassador to commemorate the 25th anniversary of the event. During the speeches at the embassy we learned that in Holland, in 1945, 1,000 people a day were dying of starvation. Each officer received a decoration and a print of the one and only photograph taken of the operation from the ground that day. I have since had the opportunity to learn much more of the terrible hardship endured by the people of that brave country during the long years of occupation and it is a source of great satisfaction to have participated a little in this effort to relieve their distress.

The Goodchild Family During the 1939–45 War

David Goodchild

The following account focuses on members of a single family, and their collective military involvement during the Second World War. This story provides a wonderful insight into how many within individual families were actively involved in the war, regardless of background or sex. Everyone had a part to play, whether in the context of home defence or in overseas action.

HAROLD GOODCHILD

My father joined the Local Defence Volunteers (L.D.V.) (later to become the Home Guard of *Dad's Army* fame), and served as the sergeant of the Toppesfield, Essex platoon where he was a local farmer, part of his land being used by RAF Bomber Command as a "decoy" airfield.

His original arm was his own 12-bore shotgun, later replaced by the Sten machine gun, a rather rudimentary but nevertheless relatively effective weapon which was mass produced at two shillings and six pence a time (12.5 pence). He died in 1965.

JOYCE GOODCHILD

My mother joined the A.R.P. (Air Raid Precautions) in 1940 and became an Air Raid Warden stationed in and around Jesus Lane in Cambridge where she very narrowly escaped harm in May or June 1940, during one of the very first German bombing raids of the war. She later moved to Sussex where she had a house in Doodle Bug Alley, where she was often kept awake by the flying bombs (V1) passing directly overhead on their way to London. She died in 1989.

My Eldest Sister, Joan MacCallum

At the outbreak of the war Joan was an operating theatre sister at St. Bartholomew's hospital, close to the Smithfield Market, in the City of London, where she had a very busy and also dangerous time during the Blitz, particularly when the Germans tried to fire-bomb the capital. My father, some 65 miles away, was able to witness these raids from far away, as the burning fires lit up the sky. Fortunately, my sister survived and later joined the Queen Alexandra's Army Nursing Service ("The Queenies") as a theatre sister with the rank of Lieutenant. She was to land at Ouistreham on the Normandy coast, some 15 days after D Day and served in the tented hospital in Bayeux to start with, following the Second Army as far as Antwerp. She then returned to the UK before being transferred to India, where she served in a base hospital looking after casualties of the jungle war in Burma and working in the operating theatre. One of the surgeons operating there was a Major in the Royal Army Medical Corps (R.A.M.C.), who commanded a paratroop ambulance unit, returning to the hospital to operate on those requiring surgical attention.

He was an American, who answered President Roosevelt's broadcast appeal in 1940 to American doctors and surgeons to come over to England to help out and he joined the R.A.M.C. in Leeds. His name was James MacCallum and he and my sister both ended up in Singapore in 1945. At the end of the war with the Japanese, they both went their separate but opposite ways to be demobilized, but by the end of 1947 they were married and went to live in America.

MY SECOND SISTER, MARGOT CAREW

Very early on in the war Margot joined the A.T.S. (Auxiliary Territorial Service) and trained at the Royal Artillery Anti-Aircraft School in Manorbier near Pembroke in South Wales where she was later on to be commissioned, finishing the war as a Lieutenant.

She served in a number of anti-aircraft batteries stationed in places like Dagenham in Essex and Hyde Park in London, where a fellow officer was Mary Churchill, later to become Lady Soames, who came to Paris later on with her husband, Christopher, as our Ambassador.

Margot eventually left the A.T.S. before the end of the war, after marrying Major Thomas Carew, and they eventually ended up in Quetta in the north-west part of what is now known as Pakistan, where he commanded a Royal Artillery Para Light Regiment.

Thomas, a regular soldier in 1938, led a remarkable war, being stationed in Gibraltar at the outbreak and getting very bored because nothing ever seemed to happen. In 1940, he returned to the UK to join the forces in Narvik in Norway, only to be pushed out by the German Army pretty quickly and finding himself back in Gibraltar a few weeks later to become bored again.

Boredom was finally brought to an end when he volunteered to return to England to join the Jedburgh units created, I believe, by the famous Colonel Buckmaster. They consisted of small groups of an English or American officer with a French liaison officer and an English or American wireless operator sergeant. They were parachuted into France to prepare and help the French Resistance for the eventual invasion in June 1944 and later to impede the Germans sending up reinforcements. Thomas was decorated with the Croix de Guerre and the Légion d'Honneur for his work in France before leaving to be dropped behind the Japanese lines in Burma, where he had a number of rather harrowing experiences, reaching the rank of Brigadier for a few months to deal with persuading a Burmese tribe to change allegiances. Thomas received a number of British decorations, I believe the DSO, the MC, and a mention in dispatches. He eventually retired from the peacetime Army to build boats in Chichester.

My sister went out to live in Fuengirola in Southern Spain when it was just a small and most attractive fishing village. She was to die as a result of a road accident in Surrey off the Hog's Back in 1970.

MY BROTHER, JOHN GOODCHILD, DECEASED 1943

John tried his best to join the Army as soon as war broke out but, being told he was too young, he then volunteered to be a rear-gunner with the R.A.F. who never got around to calling him up. He then found out he could join the Army after all as a regular for 5 years which he proceeded to do and joined the Suffolk Regiment in Bury St. Edmunds.

After scant training he was sent to defend the Norfolk beaches after Dunkirk where - armed with an assortment of weapons, some of the soldiers having none at all - they were supposed to stop a German invasion. After the scare was over his Regiment continued its training up in Hawick in the Scottish borders and was then sent to Liverpool to clear up bomb damage.

The Regiment was part of the Army's 18th Division (known as the East Anglian Division) and left Liverpool for the Western Desert. However it never got there as the Japanese invaded Malaya in December 1942 following the attack on Pearl Harbour and the Prime Minister decided it should be sent instead to Singapore after a few weeks of jungle training in India to bolster up its defence.

The Division arrived in Singapore just 48 hours before its surrender and the Regiment put up a spirited but forlorn show of defiance; its survivors were marched off to the Changi prison on the Island.

My brother and many of his comrades were taken up to the River Kwai where they were put to work on the infamous railway in conditions that we all know were quite horrendous and cruel. My brother, after a number of attacks of dysentery and malaria with no or little medicine available to treat him, finally succumbed and died on the 11th October 1943 at the age of 22. His remains were finally buried in the rather wonderful and well kept military cemetery beside the river which my family and I had the honour of visiting in 1976.

After the war my mother received many letters from his commanding officers attesting both to his bravery in battle and forbearance in captivity and that he might well have received the Military Medal (M.M.) had he survived.

MYSELF, DAVID GOODCHILD

I volunteered to join the Army in February 1944 whilst still at school, and effectively did in July. After training as a gunner in the Royal Artillery, I was commissioned and sent off to India in 1946. There I served with the 4th Indian Field Regiment (all Muslims) and the 2nd Indian Field Regiment (all Sikhs) as a Battery Command Officer (C.P.O.), both regiments being equipped with 25 powder self propelled guns known as Sextons.

After helping out during the period prior to Independence Day in August 1947 and afterwards, I returned to England and was demobilized in February 1948.

One of my cousins died as a fighter pilot in the R.A.F., another in a Yeomanry Regiment was killed in Burma and a third in the Royal Artillery was decorated with the M.C. for his bravery in the Western Desert in North Africa.

To Hell with that!

Oliver Gyles Longley

Gyles Longley, like many of his contemporaries, joined the war at a reasonably young age and was involved in many of the well known theatres of conflict, as can be gleaned from the following account. Indeed, his was a very interesting, diverse and very respectable military career during the war. I have had the pleasure of knowing Gyles since I was about 14. When I was 17, Gyles kindly lent me his dress medals as a stage prop supporting my incarnation as Colonel Pickering, in the musical "My Fair Lady". I have always been very proud to know Gyles, and the following excerpt was kindly donated from his book of the same title.

En route for Egypt (May 1942 – July 1942)

After embarkation leave, our vehicles were driven to Liverpool to load onto cargo ships, whilst we took the train to Gourock in Scotland to board an American liner, the *Santa Elena*. The crew were American, supported by elements of the American Navy to man the gun with which the ship was armed. Unlike British ships, all American ships under military control are dry so there was no hope of any alcoholic refreshment during our voyage. However, it was said the only person on board who enjoyed a drink was the American barber, who imbibed the bay rum hair freshener normally reserved for his customers. The *Santa Elena* had been a luxury cruise ship part of an American cruise line fleet, which in peacetime operated on the Pacific coast from San Francisco down to Mexico. It was not built for Atlantic gales. It was a small liner designed to carry only a few hundred passengers. It had been adapted to take nearly two thousand troops so conditions, particularly for the men, were not very comfortable. Extra sleeping accommodation had been built up over the decks to provide for sleeping in hammocks. Meals were American style, everything on the plate topped up with ice cream and with a cup of coffee. There were only two meals a day which were taken standing up. It was necessary to have several successive meal sessions throughout the day to be able to cater for everyone.

The officers fared rather better. We had our own dining room and in my case I shared a cabin with five other officers in bunks two abreast on three levels.

As part of the 44th Home Counties Division, we sailed in a very large convoy at the end of May 1942. I understand it was one of the largest ever, comprising several ocean liners, a battleship (*HMS Rodney*, after he exploits with the Bismarck and a refit in the US), cruisers, an aircraft carrier and destroyers. Attending the troop carrying liners was *RMS Aquitania*.

It was with some apprehension I watched the changing scene as we sailed down the River Clyde from Gourock to join our convoy in the open sea. Once formed, the convoy sailed due west for several days before turning south in order to give the French coast a very wide berth.

The weather in the North Atlantic was atrocious. I am a good sailor, so I was one of the few who did not suffer from seasickness. I often wonder how I could have survived the stench when inspecting the troops' sleeping quarters. It was also pretty bad in our cramped cabin.

Our constant fear was to be attacked by submarines. During the day the convoy was spread over a vast area

– a magnificent sight for me, who loved anything to do with ships. At night, with total black-out, the convoy closed up to avoid scattering and becoming separated, which would have been a gift for a German submarine. Night navigation was tricky and dangerous between ships, being close together with only a small dimmed light shining at the stern of each ship. There were some narrow misses.

Before we left Britain we had been issued with tropical kit including sun helmets so we naturally assumed we were destined for the Far East theatre. As Singapore had fallen in February 1942 there was a potential Japanese threat to India. However shortly after leaving Britain it was announced we would be going to Egypt. On board training and lectures, so far as possible, were then directed to preparing us for this destination.

The trip lasted nearly two months with a stop for refuelling at Freetown in Sierra Leone but we were not permitted to disembark. We remained anchored there for several days in the blistering heat until the convoy set sail for South Africa. Half the convoy, including the *Santa Helena* docked at Capetown, whilst the other half went on to Durban. Capetown is a magnificent setting, overshadowed by Table Mountain. We were able to disembark and spent three glorious days there, royally entertained by the South African people. The voyage to South Africa had been uneventful from air and submarine attack thanks to the wonderful naval protection.

We left Capetown at breakfast time one morning and immediately encountered the enormous waves prevalent on rounding the Cape. Our breakfast shot across the dining room and for the next few days it was not possible to provide any hot meals for the entire ship. For anyone who has not experienced this type of sea these waves which seem like mountains are frightening. Anything movable went crashing all over the ship.

After a while things quietened down, meals were restored as we sailed up the east coast of Africa. From Capetown onwards our naval escort was much reduced, no battleship, no aircraft carrier, just a few destroyers. We were a little nervous though, as Japanese submarines were reported to be operating in the Indian Ocean.

Having left Britain in late May, the 44th Division duly arrived safely at Port Tewfik at the southern entrance to the Suez Canal in late July 1942.

NORTH AFRICA (JULY 1942 – SEPTEMBER 1943)

After disembarkation at Port Tewfik we travelled by train to an area between Alexandria and Cairo where we started training to become acclimatised for desert warfare. We were there for only two weeks before being ordered to the Alamein line in reserve. On arrival in Egypt we had quickly discarded our tropical helmets as unsuitable headgear. But in the desert we also found our motor cycles and L.R.C.s (light reconnaissance cars) were equally unsuitable and discarded them in favour of jeeps and other scout cards.

At the time of our arrival in Egypt, the German General Erwin Rommel and his Afrika Corps together with the Italian Army, had been halted along the Alamein line. This stretched from the coast to the impenetrable Quatarra Depression some forty miles to the south. The British Forces in the Middle East were commanded by General Claude Auchinleck with General Ritchie in command of the 8th Army. However Churchill had lost faith with Auchinleck and Ritchie. He wanted General Gott to take over the 8th Army; unfortunately he was killed in an air accident. Churchill then decided to make a complete change and relieved Auchinleck of his command, to be replaced by my "hero", General Alexander, to command the Middle East and General Bernard Montgomery to command the 8th Army. Monty officially took over on 15th August 1942 although he had assumed command a few days before then. He had quickly summed up the situation, saying it would not be long before Rommel would attack again, so he decided to reinforce the Alam Halfa ridge by bringing up the 44th Division.

44 Recce moved off from its camp near Cairo on 14th August and drove into the desert for the first time. I was detailed to drive off in advance to contact the headquarters of the 7th Armoured Division, the original famous "Desert Rats", so named as their divisional emblem was a jerboa, or desert rat. I was to become the liaison officer attached to this division so drove off along a desert track leaving a cloud of dust in my wake. Before long I was met by a jeep coming from the opposite direction stirring up a similar cloud of dust. When we each lowered our sand glasses to my surprise I met, in the middle of nowhere, my old Gestetner colleague, Pym Ormrod. He directed me to 7th Armoured Division where we parted company, vowing to meet for a drink at a convenient moment later but we never met up again.

On arrival I was attached to the headquarters of 22 Armoured Brigade, a part of 7th Armoured. It was not long before I was given a message to take to Lieutenant-Colonel "Stinker" Braithwaite commanding 44 Recce. I was provided with an armoured scout car with two drivers to take me there. They lost the way and got bogged down in the sand. Determined to carry out my first active service mission I left my scout car to find my way on foot. Darkness fell, I got lost, and finally came across a truck with a sergeant who could not help me but invited me to spend the night in his truck.

I awoke the next morning to find I was only a few yards from where I was supposed to be. I duly delivered my message which turned to be not very important after all. Imagining I could find my way by the stars I soon learned they moved causing one to round in a circle. My first desert lesson.

I returned to the 22nd Brigade headquarters where the Brigade Major was quite amused by my failure and lent me a jeep to go and look at the Quatarra Depression. I drove off chasing a gazelle on the way. The depression is an immense area below sea level and quite an amazing moonlike sight, considered impassable for military or any vehicle.

Unfortunately when I returned from this little jaunt my stomach was turning and I felt very sick. The Brigade Major took one look at me and had me evacuated to a hospital in the Delta where I was diagnosed with dysentery. During my absence Rommel, as expected, attacked the Alma Halfa ridge on 31st August, meeting stronger resistance than he had expected. 44 Division infantry suffered casualties in this encounter. 44 Recce was not heavily involved in this battle but nevertheless I missed my regiment's first encounter with the enemy.

After discharge from hospital I was sent to convalesce at Lady MacMichael's convalescent home in Jerusalem. Lady MacMichael was the wife of the British High Commissioner for Palestine. Whilst there I was able to visit most of the Holy places in Jerusalem and its surroundings. We spent much time with fellow convalescents drinking tomato juice at the Y.M.C.A. across the valley from the King David Hotel as we were forbidden alcohol.

In early October 1942 I finally returned to rejoin 44 Recce which was preparing for the forthcoming Battle of Alamein.

EL ALAMEIN (23RD OCTOBER 1942)

The Regiment, now under the command of Lieutenant-Colonel Lyon Corbett-Winder, was still attached to 22nd Armoured Brigade. During my absence a special task force had been formed which was named the "44th Reconnaissance Carrier Force". The role of this force was to clear and lead the way through both the British and enemy minefields as soon as the artillery barrage stopped. It consisted of four separate columns each comprising the regiment's carriers, together with those of other units, preceded by a Valentine tank specially fitted with flails to set off mines. It also included members of the Royal Engineers, whose task was to probe for and clear any mines not set off by the tanks and carriers. Some of the carriers were fitted with a sort of harrow which they dragged along behind them to set off mines and to widen the cleared lanes. Once these columns had cleared the lanes through the minefields the plan was for the Royal Scots Greys to break through with their tanks.

As the operation would be taking place at night there was intensive training through most October nights. By this time I was second in command of B squadron commanded by Major Pat Nesbitt. As such I was in reserve for the battle but took part in the rehearsals to be ready to replace any officer unable to do so through sickness or injury. The role of these officers was to give directions to the Valentine tank commander on a compass bearing whilst sitting behind the tank's turret. Not a very enviable task.

Monty's plan for the forthcoming battle was to make the enemy believe the main trust would come from the South. Elaborate arrangements were made to deceive the enemy. Hundreds of dummy tanks and other vehicles were assembled; dummy tracks, pipe lines and ammunition were laid out. These dispositions were carried out in secret, but as the Desert Air Force had overwhelming mastery of the skies it largely kept enemy reconnaissance planes away.

Thanks to reinforcements and a liberal supply of recently arrived American Stuart and Sherman tanks, the 8th Army was in a strong position whilst the Axis German/Italian forces were somewhat weaker and suffering from a shortage of petrol supplies. The Air Force and Navy had sunk many of Rommel's supplies. Nevertheless it was still going to be a tough job to defeat them.

On the eve of the battle, which took place on 23rd October, Monty issued an inspiring Order of the Day which was distributed to all troops.

Order of the Day, 23 October 1942

The battle which is now about to begin will be one of the decisive battles of history. The eyes of the whole world will be on us, watching anxiously which way the battle will swing. We give them their answer at once, 'It will swing our way'.

We have first-class equipment; good tanks; good anti-tank guns; plenty of artillery and plenty of ammunition; and backed by the finest air striking force in the world.

All that is necessary is that each one of us, every officer and man, should enter this battle with the determination to see it through – to fight and to kill – and finally, to win.

If we do this, there can only be one result – together we will hit the enemy for 'Six', right out of Africa.

The sooner we win the battle, which will be the turning point of the war, the sooner we shall all get back home to our families. Therefore let every officer and man enter the battle with a stout heart, and the determination to do his duty so long as he has breath in his body.

'AND LET NO MAN SURRENDER SO LONG AS HE IS UNWOUNDED AND CAN FIGHT'.

Let us pray that 'the Lord mighty in battle' will give us victory.
                    Lieutenant General Bernard Montgomery

There was complete silence in this calm moonlit evening as we waited for the barrage to start. I was about to return to my reserve position and on my way passed the Royal Scots Greys with their tanks lined up to go forward when a solitary piper in full Highland dress played his bagpipes whilst marching up and down the lines. A stirring moment I shall never forget.

At precisely 21h 40, 882 field and medium artillery guns opened up a furious barrage all along the 40 miles front from Alamein to the Quatarra Depression. It went on for twenty minutes, then the guns concentrated on specific targets. During this time the four columns of our special force moved forward. They met much stronger resistance, and many more mines, than anticipated. None of the columns managed to penetrate the mine fields except Pat Nesbitt's column which got half-way through. Casualties were heavy but Pat managed to stay on under constant and heavy fire throughout the following day. He was awarded a very well deserved D.S.O. I went up to see him during the day, he was his usual calm self, in total control of the situation. Casualties in officers and men were very high.

Rommel had been ill on sick leave at home in Germany when the battle started but returned hurriedly to take command again. To a large extent the effort in the South did succeed in causing the Axis forces to hesitate before realising the main thrust was in the North. Then the Germans, largely due to lack of transport, left the Italians to their fate in the south. The battle of Alamein lasted for twenty days before Rommel withdrew to set up a new defensive position further back.

Our engagement was called off after the breakthrough in the North when we regrouped again as 44 Recce. We pursued the Italians for about 70 miles, capturing them by the hundreds. It was a pitiful sight, as they were without food and particularly without water. In desperation they had drunk all the water from their vehicle radiators.

44 Recce was then withdrawn into reserve to a camp at Mena House just nearby the Great Pyramids. In January 1943 we moved to Cairo, stations in the Citadel, as troops to protect the General Headquarters (GHQ). This was quite a pleasant job, but necessary as King Farouk was very much pro-German.

Apart from our military duties we were able to enjoy becoming members of the exclusive Gezira country club on an island on the Nile. I also took the opportunity to listen to some excellent concerts by the Cairo Symphony Orchestra. We enjoyed the famous Shepherd's Hotel, and some excellent restaurants. Alas, it did not last long. In February we came under orders to join the 56th London Division with PAI-Force (Persia and Iraq) since there was always the possibility that the Germans might invade those countries for their oil, should the Soviets be defeated in the battle for Stalingrad. That city held until the Germans were finally defeated in February 1943.

Although we came under command of 56th Division at this time we never joined them in Iraq. Instead we were posted to the Gaza area of Palestine for training. On March 24th 1943 the division was ordered westwards to move overland to join the 8th Army, which had broken through the Mareth Line to push the enemy into Tunisia. 44 Recce left Palestine on the 28th March to meet up with 56 Division. We made the long journey by road through Sinai, Egypt, and Libya to arrive at Enfidaville in Tunisia about 24th April.

As we entered the town we were subjected to heavy shelling, something we did not greatly appreciate after the rather soft time we had been having since Alamein. Until the German surrender, on 13th May, fighting was very intense, particularly in the hills near Tunis, and 44 Recce was very actively engaged. By then I had rejoined B squadron, which was still commanded by Pat Nesbitt until he was sent to Staff College. He was replaced by Major Alec Hambro. It was not long before Alec was severely wounded, so I had to take over in the middle of the battle when we were continually under fire. As soon as possible after the battle I went to see Alec in hospital. He seemed quite cheerful but, sadly, died shortly after. Another fellow officer, slightly senior to me, was appointed to succeed Alec to command the squadron but he declined so I was then given command of the squadron and promoted to Major.

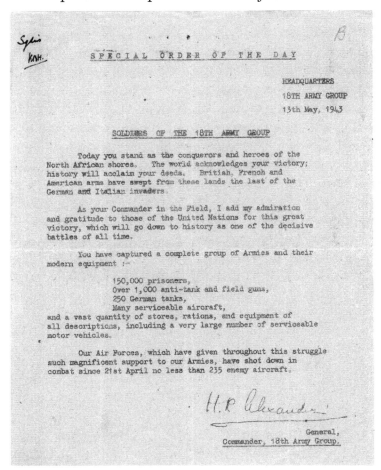

Order of the Day, 13 May 1943

To celebrate the Allied victory a Victory Parade was held in Tunis taken by General Alexander, accompanied by General Montgomery and others from the Anglo-American Army which had landed in Algeria under "Operation Torch" to attack the enemy's west flank. 44 Recce then returned to Tripoli to prepare for the Italian Campaign.

LIFE IN THE WESTERN DESERT AND EGYPT

The advantage of war in the Western Desert was that apart from each side trying to overcome the other, the sand and the rocks suffered, as compared with, later in Italy, towns and villages and their occupants.

The desert had its attractions. Away from the noise of battle a deep and mysterious, almost spiritual, silence prevailed over this vast, never-ending, area of sand and rocky ground. Nevertheless there was life, the occasional struggling vegetation, the sudden display of wild flowers after rain in the spring, the sight of a fleeting gazelle, the charming lazy chameleon until it shot out its long tongue with lightning speed to trap its prey, the strange dung beetle rolling balls of dung to its nest in the sand.

One had to be aware of scorpions, green, yellow and black. A sting from the black scorpion is the most dangerous. I found one which had crept into my bedroll for warmth during the night. They do not sting unless provoked, or after prey. Carefully, I did not provoke mine.

The biggest curse of all were the flies. They got everywhere. It was difficult to keep them off one's food. They settled on the slightest scratch, to produce desert sores which could become sufficiently serious to merit evacuation to hospital. At certain times of the year a flock of geese or some other birds would fly over to their distant destination. Most of the time the climate was pleasantly warm but cold at nights. It could also be quite cold in winter. Sandstorms were another hazard. They were mostly dust storms which would suddenly blow up, sometimes lasting for days. It was like being in a fog. The sand and dust penetrated your clothes, food and everything else.

On the whole I liked the desert but in the beginning I missed my family and used to look up at the moon, believing that if my parents were also looking at the moon I felt there was a comforting feeling of communication between us.

Whilst we were never without water, it was scarce, so there was little available either for our daily ablutions or for the washing of clothes. From time to time, laundry would be sent to the Delta. There were also field units which sterilized our clothing. Mobile shower units were very welcome.

We always carried cans of water, using captured German jerricans if possible, but we would normally only consume this water in an emergency. One did not drink during the day, except for the inevitable brew-up of tea, but drank as much water as possible around breakfast time because drinking during the heat of day would soon be lost in sweat.

It was a gentleman's war in that both sides accepted the conventions of war. Rommel was a respected commander of the Afrika Corps who likewise respected his opponents. There were no SS battalions in the desert to disregard the Geneva Convention. We unashamedly tuned our wireless sets to listen to Lale Andersen singing the syrupy nostalgic German song "*Lilli Marlene*".

For our comforts we had to put up with Canadian Club whisky and Canadian beer. We smoked locally made Egyptian "V" for Victory Virginia cigarettes, which nearly caused a mutiny, as the troops hated them and demanded their Players or Woodbines. The authorities caved in and brought in C to C (Cape to Cairo) cigarettes

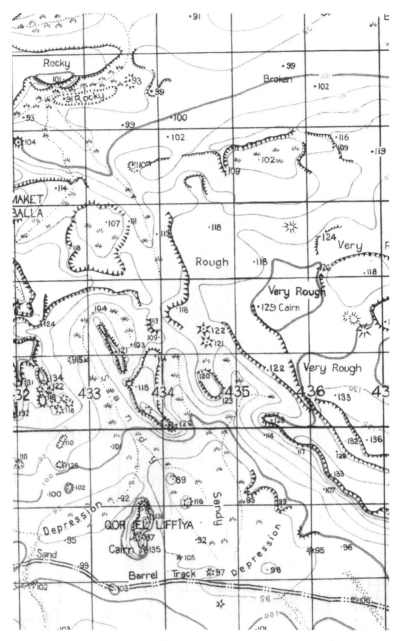

Section of 1 to 50,000 Map, drawn by South African Survey Coy in 1941, and revised by 19th Field Survey Coy in June 1942

made in South Africa. We did not care for them either so finally valuable shipping space was found to bring in our Gold Flake, Players and Woodbines from the UK.

We generally kept in good health but, in addition to desert sores, most at sometime suffered from dysentery, generally fairly mild, as was my case. Infective hepatitis, or jaundice, to which I succumbed, was quite common too and I had to spend some time in hospital. British Military Hospitals were always excellent and the nursing sisters a glad sight in this predominately male society.

From time to time there was leave. Either in Cairo, where there was plenty of entertainment, or on to the Suez Canal Zone, which had a very French flavour. On one occasion, together with other fellow officers, we took the luxury night train down to Luxor and spent some very interesting days visiting many of the famous tombs – the Valley of the Kings and the temples at Karnak. We had a wonderful Coptic Christian guide called Ghally Hana. There is something to be said for the old saying "join the army and see the world".

Pyramids, 1943. From left to right, on camels, Gyles Longley, Ted Blaber, Pat Nesbitt, Orme Gill, Dr. Smith

THE ITALIAN CAMPAIGN (10TH JULY 1943 - 2ND MAY 1945)

Wikipedia reminds me that no Campaign in Western Europe cost more than the Italian Campaign in terms of lives lost and wounds suffered by infantry forces.

Approximately 650,000 Allied, including air strength, and, on the other side, 350,000 Axis forces took part. The Allied armies comprised American, British, French, Canadian, Indian, Moroccan, Algerian, New Zealand, South African, Nepalese, and Polish units.

It is estimated that between July 1943 and May 1945, some 60,000 Allied and 50,000 German soldiers died in the Campaign, with a further 320,000 Allied casualties and 336,000 German casualties.

Prior to victory in North Africa there had been much discussion between Roosevelt and Churchill on the best strategy to defeat the Axis. Churchill was in favour of attacking the under-belly of Europe through Italy pending the eventual invasion of Northern Europe, whilst Roosevelt wanted all the Allied effort to concentrate on the invasion of Northern Europe planned for 1943, which would weaken the German pressure on the Soviet front. However this could only be achieved by winning the Battle of the Atlantic first.

Eventually the US and British political leadership took the decision to put off the invasion of France until early 1944 and instead to commit the large trained Allied forces in the Mediterranean to a lower priority Italian campaign. This hopefully might lead to eliminating Italy from the war as well as enable the Allied Navies, principally the British Navy, and the Allied Air Forces to complete their domination of the Mediterranean Sea, thereby massively improving communications with Egypt, the Middle East, the Far East and India. It would also cause the Germans and Italians to transfer troops from the Eastern front to defend Italy and southern France, thus aiding the Soviet Union.

The plan was first to invade Sicily to be followed by the invasion of Italy.

Operation Husky to capture Sicily took place from 10th July to 17th August 1943 with a force of 160,000 Allied forces. Although the Axis forces were beaten, the Germans nevertheless managed to evacuate some 60,000 troops and much of their material across the Messina Straits to the Italian mainland.

We did not take part in the Sicilian campaign. At the time I was still commanding "B" Squadron, 44 Recce under command of Lieutenant-Colonel Kenneth Hicks. We were stationed near Tripoli in Libya from May to September, to plan and get ready for the forthcoming invasion of Italy. We were still a part of 56 Division, which in turn was a part of 10th Army Corps commanded by Lieutenant-General Brian Horrocks. One of Monty's favourite generals, he was always full of enthusiasm and energy. As was his custom, he came to visit us to give us a pep talk and to explain his future plans. One of his favourite expressions was to ask if we had the "light of battle" in our eyes. Seemingly we must have given him satisfaction, as he did not berate us for any lack of such light. Keeping those under one's command fully informed of one's plan is an essential part of winning their confidence and in this Horrocks was quite an expert.

Preparations for the invasion included taking mepacrine pills against malaria. Malaria-carrying mosquitoes were very prevalent in certain parts of Italy. It was necessary to take these pills every day. They turned our skin yellow, rather like jaundice. The troops did not like that so it was necessary to adopt a strict discipline when the orderly officer had to ensure they take them at meal times. It was not easy to make sure they had actually swallowed them. Obviously many did not, resulting in a serious number of malaria cases later on, throughout all the forces, after landing in the malaria infested Salerno area.

All our vehicles had to be waterproofed, as they would very likely have to drive through water on disembarking from the landing craft, L.C.T.s (Landing Craft Tanks). These ships, specially designed for the purpose, could carry all my squadron plus a few other troops. They were able to come into shallow water to let down their ramps for the vehicles to drive off.

As the Germans had been defeated in Sicily, it was thought the chosen area for the landings in the Bay of Salerno, south of Naples, would not present great opposition. However, at a briefing just prior to embarkation we were told that the Germans had moved in further new formations. I did not feel so confident that it would be a walk-over after that.

Before sailing General Horrocks was injured in an air raid on Tripoli. Although he recovered later he did not take part in the Italian campaign. He was succeeded by Lieutenant-General Richard (Dick) McCreery.

In between periods of training and preparation I managed to get away to visit the magnificent well-preserved ruins of the old Roman cities – second century B.C. Sabratha and Leptis Magna. These cities on the coat of Tripolitania were originally founded by the Carthaginians in the fifth century B.C.

SALERNO, 9TH SEPTEMBER 1943

I was now about to take part in the Italian Campaign, in which my Regiment served with distinction, although we were not directly involved in most of the most intensive major battles such as Monte Cassino, the Anzio Landing, and the Battle for Rimini. These were some of the fiercest during all the war. Although the Allies were greatly superior in numbers the Germans had the advantage of a series of well prepared defensive lines across the mountainous terrain, with its many rivers. Much of the time the weather was atrocious, especially in the winter, and often contributed so much delay.

Itinerary of the 44th Reconnaissance Regiment - Italian Campaign, September 1943 - December 1945

These defensive lines which had to be overcome after the Battle of Salerno were, successively, the Volturno Line, the Gustav Line, the Caesar Line, the Albert Line, the Heinrich Line and finally the Gothic Line.

As a motorised reconnaissance regiment, it was not often that we could operate as such, as the Germans systematically blew up all the bridges as they retreated. These had to be repaired or replaced rapidly by Bailey bridges – a British invention of metal sections which could be rapidly assembled by the Royal Engineers. A bridge capable of supporting tanks could be assembled overnight. As a consequence we were often employed in various roles as infantry, special task forces, or holding secondary fronts to enable other forces to mount an attack.

In this context the invasion, code-named "Avalanche", took place. My squadron embarked at Tripoli harbour and set sail to join the invasion armada of hundreds of ships of all types.

During the crossing we heard that Italy had surrendered. This was very heartening as we imagined we would then be able to sail straight into Naples. It was not quite like that, as we were reminded when a German aircraft fired on us during the night before the landings, luckily without any casualties.

The invasion of Salerno was undertaken by the 5th United States Army under U.S General Mark Clark with the British 10th Army Corps under his command. The remainder of the 8th Army, under General Montgomery, had landed in the South of Italy to move up the East coast. The 8th Army met little opposition to start with, and quickly occupied the port of Bari on the Adriatic as well as the airfields around Foggia.

All seemed quite quiet as our L.C.T. took up position in the Bay of Salerno at dawn on a magnificent calm sunny day. The massive display of hundreds of warships, different types of landing craft, and hospital ships was most impressive and reassuring. The battle commenced on 9th September. By the time we arrived, the first wave of troops had landed to secure the beachhead but had met with heavier resistance than expected.

Our role was to land with our armoured cars, carriers, and other vehicles as soon as the first wave had moved sufficiently inland. As the first wave was held up, it was not possible so we had to remain on board for a time. Out in the Bay warships were shelling the Germans who were able to oversee the armada and battle area from the mountainous hills overlooking the Salerno plain, over which the invading forces were making very slow progress. Among the warships was the gallant old *HMS Warspite*, a 1914-18 battleship, with its 15-inch guns firing into the hills. As they fired we could clearly see their enormous shells flying overhead as they seemingly made their leisurely way towards their targets.

On D+1 our turn came to move to the beach to disembark. The operation went well, without any casualties, but it was a gruesome sight to see the havoc around about, especially the effect of German flame throwers. Once ashore, my role with B squadron was to advance with my armoured cars and carriers to take over the so-called tobacco factory (which in fact was tomato canning factory) near the small town of Battipaglia, in the middle of the Salerno plain, and advance further forward with the Guards Regiment. However this was not possible as the advancing Guards and the Royal Fusiliers regiment, which had previously captured the tobacco factory, were driven out by a German counter attack. They were forced to withdraw to a rear position. As we could not move forward, we were then crammed into a field, together with units of the American army in the bridgehead area.

The whole area was infested with mosquitoes. Thanks, no doubt, to the mepacrine tablets we had been taking, the mosquito-repellent ointment with which we smeared ourselves, and the anti-mosquito bivouac tents with which we had been issued, we had few malaria casualties. However, this was not the case for some units, where the number of cases of malaria was quite high.

I chatted to two of my officers on 13th September; it was night and we were thinking of bedding down. After a while I left them to return to my command car. An enemy plane flew over, showering us with anti-personnel grenades. These flutter to the ground and explode. We suffered two casualties – unfortunately, the two officers with whom I had just been chatting. They received fatal injuries. I was lucky.

This was a great loss; by the time we had evacuated them it was quite late. I then received an order to report to regimental headquarters. The Colonel briefed me on the situation and I was ordered to reorganise my squadron to be ready to take over from the survivors of the 9th Royal Fusiliers, who had fought magnificently but had suffered heavy casualties at the front. Although we would move in with most of our vehicles, it was necessary to prepare for as many men as possible to act in an infantry role.

On my return, together with my officers and squadron Sergeant-Major, we spent the rest of the night reorganising the squadron for this unaccustomed role. At first light I made contact with the Fusiliers to reconnoitre the ground and to make arrangements to take over that evening. Having spent most of the night without any sleep, I was beginning to feel quite tired, so to refresh myself on the way back to my squadron I stopped off at a field of tomatoes. As I was indulging in eating my favourite fruit, up pops a head from the other side of a row of tomato plants to introduce himself as Colonel Twisleton-Wykenham-Fiennes, commander of the Guards regiment. I thought his name was a joke; I found out later that he came from a very distinguished military family. We ate our tomatoes and went on our respective ways.

On my return to the squadron I gathered al my officers and men around me to brief them on the situation and to issue my orders. I had quite an audience – the surrounding Americans were curious to witness a British officer giving his orders. Once this was done I was at last able to snatch a few hours' sleep.

We took over the position as planned on the evening of 14th September without any problem. Our position was quite well camouflaged in a sort of orchard of citrus fruit. The forward positions were dug in behind a farm track with a farm house on the left flank and a wooded area on the right. In front there were tomato and tobacco crops and beyond them we could see the Battipaglia tobacco factory. I made sure everyone knew their field of fire and together with my New Zealand gunnery officer, Captain "Nick" Straker, we arranged for the forward defensive fire lines to bring in fire from the guns further back in case of attack. The first night was very calm but soon after dark on the second night we could hear enemy tank movements on our front.

At dawn on 16th September we were subjected to heavy enemy shell, mortar, and machine gun fire. The shells and mortar bombs were bursting all around us. Red, green and white streams of tracer bullets were coming at us. Leaves and branches were being torn off the trees as the enemy made attempts to overwhelm us. The situation became serious so I called for intense gun fire on the advancing enemy which Nick Straker calmly directed from his forward observation position. Even the naval ships in the bay were giving us support. Our telephone lines to the forward positions were cut by the enemy gunfire and our troops wireless sets were not working well which made it difficult to control the situation so we had to resort to runners.

My command car was riddled with bullets and collapsed but its wireless was still working, enabling me to keep contact with HQ from a trench beside the vehicle. In the course of running over to contact one of the positions I dropped to the ground as I saw an advancing German trying to take a shot at me; he missed.

Whilst I was on the ground a shell burst behind me. I did not feel anything at the time but a small piece of shrapnel pierced the sole of my left boot and into the sole of my foot. I soon found it painful to walk without the support of a rifle to act as a walking stick.

The battle raged all day. One of my armoured cars was hit, setting it on fire and killing its occupants. To keep in touch with H.Q. my wireless operator, Corporal Pike, did his best to maintain contact. He was a great chap, but always when the action started, it upset his tummy, so he invariably had to clamber out to relieve himself. A brave necessity.

Eventually the enemy infiltrated our forward positions so I ordered my troops to withdraw to a position along a ditch just behind our orchard. Nevertheless, thanks to our resistance and the immense support from the guns, the enemy had suffered severe casualties and withdrew before the end of the day.

The Guards brigade commander, Brigadier Arkwright, came up as we were beginning to sort ourselves out, evacuate the wounded, and recuperate our vehicles. He congratulated us and told me to go for treatment for my wound. I was reluctant to leave my squadron as I did not feel I had been badly wounded, whereupon he gave me an order to go to the Advanced Dressing Station on the beachhead.

I was there for several days whilst they tried to find and dig out the piece of shrapnel in my foot. I found this process more painful than walking with the shrapnel in my foot, providing I was careful to avoid pressure on that part of my foot, so I discharged myself to return to my squadron. As I needed a change of clothing, I told my batman to bring me my knapsack from my armoured car which had taken a battering. (It is customary for knap-sacks to be strapped to the outside of the vehicle). When I came to put on my clean clothes and battledress they were riddled with holes and tears from all the machine gun fire and shrapnel they had received. My clothes resembled those pieces of paper from which entertainers cut out bits to form some sort of pattern. My quartermaster soon provided me with a new outfit.

Within a few days of my being wounded my family received a War Office telegram, and a little later a letter to say that the wound was not serious.

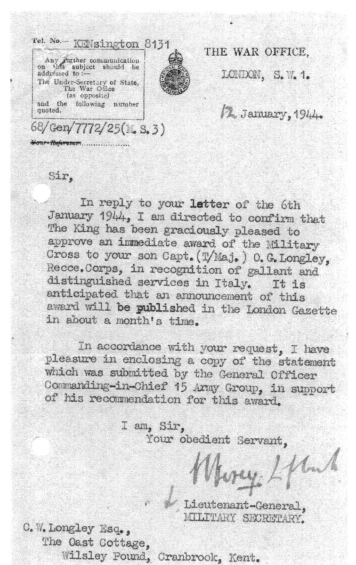

Letter to Gyles Longley's father, on his being awarded the M.C.

About two months after this action, when we had been withdrawn to prepare to join 56 Division, which had been sent to reinforce the Anzio bridgehead, I was summoned to report to the Colonel, Ken Hicks. Thinking this might concern our marching orders for Anzio I was taken to the Colonel by his batman and surprised to be greeted by him as he stood, stark naked, in a tin tub having a bath. He said, "I have something for you, Gyles", and pinned the Military Cross Brooch on my jacket. I was surprised, as I had no idea I had been recommended for an award. Naturally one is very pleased and proud but humble at the time, as one is rewarded thanks to the bravery of many and not just one person.

As I was not able to receive the medal in Italy it was sent to my family home but I received a congratulatory letter from H. M. King George VI.

For this same action; on 16th September, I had recommended my gunnery officer, Captain Nick Straker, for an award for his outstanding bravery in directing fire on the enemy whilst he was himself under constant enemy fire. I was delighted that he was also awarded an immediate M. C.

The Eighth made contact with the Fifth Army by the 18th September but already the Germans had started to withdraw from the Salerno area to their defensive line on the Volturno river.

AFTER SALERNO (OCTOBER 1943 – JULY 1944)

When I returned to my Squadron we were for a short while able to operate as a reconnaissance unit, to keep in touch with the enemy as they were retreating to the Volturno Line. Unfortunately, I was not able to take part in the crossing of the Volturno, as I was stricken with diphtheria and evacuated to the American hospital in Naples. The city had only just been captured on 1st October.

The Americans had commandeered the main hospital of Naples. As the hospital had received my medical history from the British they decided to investigate my foot whilst treating me for diphtheria. I was alarmed when they seriously suggested an operation. Luckily I was transferred to a British army hospital to complete my treatment when a nursing sister took one look at my foot and painlessly extracted a small piece of shrapnel which had worked its way to the surface. As I had for some time been walking awkwardly on the side of my foot this has caused me much trouble in later life.

In hospital in Naples I had an excellent view from my bed of Mount Vesuvius erupting. It had been erupting, shooting red hot lava into the air and covering the surrounding area with volcanic dust for some weeks. A very impressive sight at night time. Vesuvius has not erupted again since those days.

For convalescence from diphtheria I was transported by an American ambulance plane to Atania in Sicily. There was a slight hitch on arrival, as the pilot managed to clip his wing on a hanger whilst manoeuvring on the tarmac. It was not serious but a bit disturbing to watch as I lay on my stretcher in the plane. I was taken to the most delightful convalescent home at Taormina from which I was able to study the constantly smoking Mount Etna, yet another volcano.

No doubt if I were to consult the War Diaries of the 44 Recce I could give a day by day account of the Regiment as it advanced to Rome, across the Apennines to the Adriatic coast and thence on to Venice, by which time the Germans had surrendered in Italy, then on to Trieste to protect the Italian frontier from the aggressive Yugoslavia.

This would be rather boring so I will try to give an impression of what 44 Recce did and the circumstances in which we fought the Italian Campaign after Salerno.

On account of the mountainous terrain all the way up to the River Po basin in the North of the country the

Germans had the advantage of being able to establish well prepared defensive lines. Unlike the war in North Africa, which was primarily a war of movement with armoured vehicles, in Italy it was much more an infantry and artillery war, at times not dissimilar to the 1914-18 war.

As Reconnaissance regiments were not well suited to this type of warfare we were on many occasions obliged to leave our vehicles to act in an infantry role. Although we saw plenty of action we were not, except on the fringes, engaged in the heaviest battles, some of which were the bloodiest in the war. We spent much of our time on special operations, holding defensive positions, and patrolling, in addition to the occasional moments when we could deploy in our proper role. Nevertheless we were involved in many fierce clashes with the enemy and played an important role as the Allies slowly advanced up the Italian peninsula. The advance was greatly hampered by the atrocious weather, particularly in the winters of 1943 and 1944. This was an added advantage to the enemy as transport was slowed down by mud, and also by the Germans flooding the lower marshland and coastal plains. There were many rivers flowing down from the mountains which rose dramatically with the torrential rain. Naturally, as they retreated the enemy blew up all the bridges.

Although most of the time, the Allies had an overwhelming superiority in men and equipment compared with the Germans, the later had the immense advantage in a defensive war under these conditions.

Eventually the Germans abandoned the Volturno Line to take up new well-prepared positions along the Gustav Line which stretched from near Gaeta north of Naples to near Ortona on the Adriatic coast. In advancing to this new line we did manage to keep contact with the retreating enemy in small-scale actions liberating small towns and villages on the way. On one of these actions A Squadron even managed to surprise a German sapper party preparing to blow up a bridge. The sappers were captured and the bridge taken intact.

As we progressed the local population greeted us with great joy and were sometimes helpful in pointing out enemy positions. On one occasion as we had settled into a new position based on a farmhouse, I wandered down a track to see some of my men when I stepped on an S-mine. These are anti-personnel mines buried in the ground with three tiny prongs sticking out. When I heard a click, like a twig snapping, I realised I would be dead in the next second or two. The mine jumped out of the ground, glanced on my chest but miraculously failed to explode. It took me a few seconds to realise I was still alive. My luck made me quite famous for a time and even the Colonel showed some emotion on my escape from one of these deadly devices. Even today when I step on a twig and hear that crack my mind goes back to that day.

56 Division had the task of taking Monte Cassino, a hill dominating the low ground before the Garigliano river, which the Germans were holding as an outpost to their main Gustav Line defences behind the river Garigliano. The plan was to capture this hill as part of the plan to break through the Gustav Line before winter set in. For this operation elements of 44 Recce were given a new role to act as porters to supply the attacking infantry brigades, whilst others, including my B squadron, held a part of the line and patrolling. One of the Regiment's officers, Captain – later Major – Peter Osmond, a South African officer who had been seconded to us, volunteered to undertake a two-day personal patrol behind the German positions. He returned with valuable information on 30th November. A few days later he carried out a similar patrol with equal success

single-handedly killing or capturing twelve Germans. Peter was heartily congratulated by the Divisional Commander, Major-General G.W.R. Templer. He was naturally famed as an inspiration to everyone but he remained a modest and resourceful regimental officer as second in command of A squadron. When asked to explain his success his answer was that from an early age he was accustomed to tracking game in Africa when it was necessary to approach one's quarry with stealth. Tracking Germans was to him much easier. For his patrols he would take a rifle and a few rounds, a pocket full of cigarettes and a pocket full of chocolate. He was awarded the M. C.

Following the Monte Cassino event the Regiment was withdrawn to spend Christmas 1943 in reserve in the area of San Donata and Falciano.

On the 8th January 1944 the regiment returned to action as part of "Hicksforce", named after our Colonel. In addition to 44 Recce this force was reinforced by elements of other units to take over the coastal sector south of the Garigliano to carry out extensive patrolling. This lasted for about a week, during which a few prisoners were captured. We also had to contend with snipers. One morning, whilst I was shaving in the open behind a building which I thought was quite safe, a bullet smashed into the wall narrowly missing my head. I quickly went inside to finish my shave and to organise a sniper hunt, which failed to find anyone. Hicksforce was part of the plan for the main attack to cross the Garigliano in which 56 Division played an important role. This attack took place on 17th January 1944. 44 Recce crossed on foot the following day with A and C squadrons whilst B squadron was in reserve. C squadron occupied the San Salvatito feature on the left flank of the hills north of the Garigliano. They had done well but were being shot at by snipers. With B squadron

I was called in to make a sweep up the hill behind a moving artillery barrage as we clambered up. It was quite frightening as the shells started falling short. We finally made contact with Major Ted Blaber and his C squadron as he exclaimed 'about time too'.

Ignoring his taunt we passed through his lines when I gave the order to fix bayonets as we swept through to the top of the hill bayoneting bushes, and every other possible hiding place. As is often the case on such occasions we did not kill anyone as they fled as we advanced. Sadly we lost a very good young officer who was killed by our own artillery shells which were dropping short. We then returned back across the Garigliano into reserve. On account of heavy rain the river had swollen so much that the Engineers manning the pontoon bridge we had to cross feared it might be swept away any minute. Thankfully it held for us but was washed away shortly after.

B Squadron was again back in action north of the Garigliano. When supported by tanks it attacked and took a German position without loss.

Later in January we were relieved to the rear to re-organise with new vehicles, but plans were changed when we were detailed to return on foot to relieve one of the infantry regiments in the area of San Lorenzo. During February the Regiment carried out numerous patrols, captured a number of prisoners but sustained many casualties. The regiment was commended by the divisional commander for its work in its unaccustomed role acting as infantry.

The Germans fell back to their main defences on the Gustav Line, based on Monte Cassino, which dominated the route to Rome. There were four battles before the Monte Cassino position was taken. The first was in January 1944, the second in February, the third in March, and the final battle May. Those battles were some of the most costly during the war and fought successively by American, British, New Zealand, Canadian, French and Polish forces. A diversionary seaborne landing was made by American and British forces in January 1944 near Anzio, south of Rome. In anticipation the Germans had reinforced this area; another extremely costly battle raged until the final breakout in May was possible.

In February 1944, 56th Division, without 44 Recce, was withdrawn and sent to reinforce the Anzio bridgehead in early February 1944. The situation at Anzio had become very difficult. The Division fought there until the end of March when it was withdrawn to return to Egypt for rest and refit.

In the meantime 44 Recce remained in Italy and took up a defensive position west of Monte Cassino in early March 1944 from where we had an excellent view of the bombing of the mountain. It was a fantastic sight as wave after wave of bombers released their bombs but one did wonder if bombing the Monastery was right. Our role, again acting as infantry, was to hold a long line extending to the sea where we carried out a number of patrols and were subjected to a fair amount of mortaring and shelling.

One day I was taking a nap outside my headquarters when a lump of metal fell beside me with a resounding thump. It was part of a German plane which had been shot down. The pilot bailed out and landed in a tree nearby. He was in great pain with a dislocated shoulder. We managed to hoist him out of the tree and evacuate him to hospital. He was extremely young. The plus side of this incident was that I recovered his parachute and had a nice pair of silk pyjamas made from it. We were relieved by the Goums, French Moroccan troops, at the end of the month. The night before they took over, their commander, General Juin, met me to reconnoitre the position. He was a very pleasant person who went on to become a French Field Marshall. It was from here he led his fearsome Goums to make a very successful attack on Mount Cairo thus enabling the final assault on Monte Cassino by the Poles who captured it on 18th May 1944.

B

Order of the Day.
====================

by

BRIGADIER A.F.L. CLIVE, DSO. MC.

Commander 24 Gds Bde Gp

- - - - - - - - - - - - - - - - -

1.   During the past four weeks the Bde Gp has been occupying a quiet part of the Italian front. This has not necessarily meant a lazy time for all concerned, though it has not been unpleasant for the majority.

2.   A great deal of hard and sometimes dangerous work has been carried out by Battalions, accompanied often by other arms, both in alert observation and on patrol, and this is fully appreciated by the higher commanders.

3.   I wish particularly to mention the patrols of No 2 Coy 5 Gren Gds, of KW 180 to Monte ARUNCA, and of No 4 Coy 3 Coldm Gds beyond ALFADENA. All these are deserving of high praise. Good patrolling can only be successfully accomplished by brave and determined men.

4.   Now that the offensive in Italy is about to begin again, and in spite of the fact that we are, for the time being, only onlookers, we must be prepared at any moment to play our part whether it be passive or active; AND WE MUST NEVER RELAX. Only thus shall we play our part in hastening the victory which we all want and of which we shall ever be proud.

Brigadier.

In the Fd.
11 May 1944.

Order of the Day, 11 May, 1944

After being relieved by the French we went into reserve and training during which time we received our new armoured cars and hite half tracks, some of the latter being equipped with 75mm guns. We thus acquired our own self propelled artillery battery of six guns.

Rome was occupied by the Allies on 4th June, two days before the Allied landings in Normandy. In the meantime 56 Division had been withdrawn to Egypt to refit. 44 Recce did not withdraw to Egypt until a little later. In the meantime we had the opportunity to visit Rome and to attend a soldiers' audience with Pope Pius XII at the Vatican. I was privileged to sit at the feet of his Holiness and found him to be very simple and dignified. We chatted about England which he knew well as he had previously been the Papal Nuncio to Britain.

In June it was now our turn to go to Egypt for rest and training. For the voyage to Egypt I was detailed with my squadron to proceed to the South of the country to Taranto to pick up two thousand German prisoners of war and transport them by ship to Alexandria. Together with a few extra troops I had about a hundred and twenty men, plus my officers, to guard them on this trip and safely deliver them to a prisoner of war camp in Egypt. We also had a number of German officer prisoners and allowed them to have some freedom aboard but on parole on the understanding they did not communicate with their soldiers. They respected this order which was convenient and avoided having to place them under guard.

The prisoners were from German units which had fought so well at Monte Cassino. They were tough and determined to make themselves difficult which they certainly did. The ship was overcrowded making it necessary to organise them into three groups. Whilst one group had their meals, another would have access to exercise on deck whilst the third were confined to their sleeping quarters. They did their best to try to disorganise this system. There was an incident when they accused us of breaking the Geneva Convention by giving them inferior bread to eat because it was white from which all goodness had been extracted. We had to convince them we fed our own troops with this lovely white bread and that under the Geneva Convention we were obliged to provide them with the same food as our own men.

After a few days at sea, we arrived and docked at Alexandria. We remained on board for the night but when we were about to disembark the following morning two prisoners were found to be missing. They had slid down the ropes to escape to an island. Fortunately they were picked up by some Egyptians and brought back on board. We then, in accordance with the Kings Army Regulations, had hold to a Court of Inquiry. The two prisoners who appeared before the Inquiry were without boots as they had discarded them on escaping. So, again invoking the Geneva Convention, they refused to cooperate unless we provided them with boots, not something normally available for this type of situation, but somehow we managed. I was relieved when later that day we handed over the required number, signed for by the prison camp commander. We returned to Italy in July 1944.

My Life in England

John H. Konirsch

After France and Great Britain conceded the Sudetenland to Hitler and his stooges in September 1938, many Czechs sought to flee their native Czechoslovakia. John Konirsch recalls the refuge he and his sister were to gain in England. In 1945, he joined the British Army. In later years he was to find out the full extent of the inhumanity inflicted upon many of his countrymen, including to his own family, at the behest of the Nazis.

The following takes place after leaving my home town in Czechoslovakia in September 1938, after the dreadful decision by France and England in Munich, Germany, in the presence of Hitler and Mussolini, to abandon the Sudeten to the Nazis. We went to Prague with just the clothes we were wearing. My father had been mobilized. My mother, my little sister who was nine years of age, and I aged 12, arrived after several hours on a train, with thousands of other refugees. We were first offered soup by the Red Cross and later found a place to sleep at the Y.W.C.A., (Young Women's Christian Association). We spent several weeks there in a hall with many other refugees.

In 1939 on 10th March, five days before the Nazis occupied the rest of Bohemia and Moravia, (Slovakia was declared an independent State), my sister and I left by plane for the UK. England was the only country that accepted refugee children. We left Prague at 11 in the morning in a snowstorm, landed in Rotterdam for refuelling and arrived over England in beautiful sunshine. The plane flew low over Kent towards Croydon. Looking out of the window we saw little houses, clean streets with traffic lights at the crossings; it was as if we had arrived in Paradise. Thanks to the Quakers and a Christian Mission in Prague we were saved, without knowing if we would ever see our parents again.

In England we were separated during several months living in two separate children's homes. In September, the war broke out. From January 1940 we could not attend school any more. After the fall of France in June 1940 we suffered from the bombing by the Nazi planes. The house I lived in was in Chislehurst, Kent, which was on the route taken by enemy planes to bomb London. I witnessed several dog-fights by British fighter planes against the German bombers.

In December 1940 I was sent via London to Cirencester, Gloucestershire. Crossing London, which was still burning from the night bombings, I managed to get from Charing Cross Station to Paddington Station. In Cirencester I started working in a draper's shop. Several times I was designated to do fire-watching on the roof of the shop after shop hours until 1 am when a grown-up took over. My employer was very kind to me and lodged me with his family.

In 1942 my parents who had managed to escape to England, made me go and live with them in London. I went to the Polytechnic School in London, where I learned to become a tailor. In 1944 I started with a tailor in the West End. In July, at the age of 18, I was called up by the Czech Army in England. I preferred to volunteer for the British Army, and was called up on 1st March 1945.

The first few weeks were spent training in the Pioneer Corps, like all foreigners, later assigned to different Corps, as required by the Army. I was transferred to the Royal Army Service Corps (R.A.S.C.). We were preparing to leave for the Far East Centre of Operations against the Japanese. Preparations were made to select young soldiers for the different tasks. We were to leave England by August.

In the meantime we were stationed in Woking, Surrey, where I was responsible for keeping hot water for the showers. Every evening I had to scrape the ovens and at four in the morning light a new fire under the water tanks. That left me with plenty of spare time during the day, and I often went to London to see my parents. The news from Europe was excellent, and we knew that the end was near. In our minds we were grateful to the Royal Family, Mr. Churchill and the British people for having saved our lives. If not we might have shared the concentration camps with many other fellow countrymen.

Soon we were to see the final phase of the war. The Allied Armies were steadily progressing into Germany, for now the situation was reversed. Hitler ordered his stooges, the SS, to burn everything, and even to shoot people that were willing to surrender. He wanted to destroy the German people with him into the defeat. Victory in Europe was approaching and on May 8th 1945 Germany signed the unconditional surrender to the Allied Armies in the West, led by General Eisenhower.

On VE day I was on leave in London: what a wonderful day for the British people, who had suffered so much. With thousands of very happy people, I went to Piccadilly Circus, which was nearby the famous Rainbow Club where the greatest American Bands played for their soldiers. Later the crowd proceeded towards Buckingham Palace to celebrate and to salute

John Konirsch, sitting on the left with his comrades.

the King and Queen, with the two Princesses and Mr. Churchill, thanks to whose courage and determination the war was won by the Allies.

There was a dark side for me and the refugees from Czechoslovakia, Poland, Hungary and other East European countries. The Red Army occupied those countries, and although the Communists promised free elections, we did not know at the time, that it would take many years before this became true. Again Czechoslovakia had been abandoned, this time to Stalin instead of Hitler. At the conference of Yalta, the American President Roosevelt was very ill and acceded to Stalin's demand on hegemony over these countries. Mr. Churchill was the only lucid statesman, knowing that with Stalin, the whole of Europe could come under the Communist rule.

For me it was not until 1991, 42 years after I had left the country of my birth, that I managed to visit, together with my sister, the town where we were born, only to learn that some of my family had been interned in the Concentration Camp of Therezienstadt, and that my grandmother had been burned there in the infamous stoves. My grandfather had been arrested and tortured by the Gestapo and had died before being sent to the KZ (concentration camp). He was buried in the village they had lived for 20 odd years. His grave could not be located because the cemetery had been neglected and the grass had overgrown the graves.

The second part of my war service started in August 1945. I was on a ship *en route* to India. Due to the Atomic bombs over Japan, the war ended and the troopship was held up in Port Said where we all disembarked. After several days in a transit camp, I was sent to Tobruk, an R.A.S.C. petrol depot. There the Commanding Officer was pleased to have someone who could speak German, because most of the repair work was done by German P.O.W.s, all volunteers. Some pretended not to understand English. After that there was no more excuse.

Demobilisation started almost immediately, and the personnel that worked in the office, were replaced by the newcomers. After only a few weeks I was promoted to Warrant Officer Second Class (WO II). The problem of replacement at HQ R.A.S.C. was the same, and a Chief Clerk was needed and I was the only WO II available. I was transferred to HQ Petrol Supply R.A.S.C. MELF, stationed at the time in Fayed on the Bitter Lakes. I worked there until February 1948, when I was designated to repatriate several hundred German P.O.W.s. We crossed the Mediterranean by ship and came through the channel up to the estuary of the Elbe until I was demobilized.

Having done three years war service, my rank remained as War/Substantive WO II R.A.S.C.

Fishing

Djamil Jacir

The following account, provided by Colonel Jacir, is quite frankly one of the more amusing stories to emerge from what was otherwise a rather grim chapter in the history of mankind. Colonel Jacir, together with his comrades, came over to Great Britain with Charles de Gaulle and the Free French forces and spent a certain amount of time training for what was to come later in the War. As with everyone in Britain during the war (civilian and military), food was heavily rationed and scarce. This charming account depicts one reasonably novel way of how the Colonel and his comrade attempted to combat this relative hunger.

It was in 1943 that, as a member of the recently formed SAS, I was on manoeuvres in Scotland. The survival course involved iron rations of which the main element was pemmican, a source of food distinguished more by its dietetic than its gastronomic appeal. We were an inventive group (after all it was one of the qualities we were chosen for) and it didn't take long to discover that trinitrotoluene made an excellent fire lighter, provided one did not include a detonator, when all one had was a heap of wet bracken getting wetter by the minute in the rain. The end of the salmon season had been good to us and I can recommend camouflage netting as an impromptu tool for the military poacher.

Grilled salmon made a nice change from the awful pemmican based rations.

The end of the salmon season came, however, and one cold winter's morning we decided to try another means of procuring a little more palatable protein. We had an inflatable boat and pushed it out onto the nearby loch. There was one of those strange fogs which hang low over the water; if you stood up you could see for yards. When you sat down the horizon closed in to the end of the boat, the fog as thick as woodbine smoke in a N.A.A.F.I. bar.

We headed out into deep water and took out a lump of explosive (there was no shortage of that at least) and a 2m pencil detonator. Throwing it into the loch we rowed back to shore as fast as possible. We were only halfway there, however, when it went off, the explosion showering us and the landscape with pieces of wood and bits of fish flesh, none however in anything approaching edible condition. Some of the bits of fish did seem rather large, however, and encouraged surprised, as well as disparaging comments from our disappointed fellows but it was only later that I learned that this loch was special. They had said it was called Loch Ness, indeed it was marked as such on the map, but nobody had thought fit to enlighten the French contingent of the existence of a monster. Still less did the map, old as it was, say "monsters be here".

I fear the worst and pangs of guilt haunt me still as I peruse the newspapers in the news-less summer "silly season" when articles crop up about yet another expedition coming up with "No concrete evidence to prove the existence of an exceptionally large life-form in the loch."

I'm sorry if nobody's seen it since 1943, but you must understand. It wasn't really my fault, and we were awfully hungry.

Part 4: Epilogue: Post-War Accounts

epilogue
[ep-uh-lawg, -log]

noun

a concluding part added to a literary work.

Origin:
1375–1425; late Middle English epiloge < Latin epilogus < Greek epílogos peroration of a speech, equivalent to epi- epi- + lógos word

Run ashore in Holland

The Royal Navy Cold War Era (1970s)

Stephen Morris

Stephen Morris began his military career in the Royal Navy from a very young age; he enjoyed a very rewarding career and indeed got to see a great deal of the World. In his own way, like many of his contemporaries, he played his own part in various conflicts from episodes in the Cold War to other conflicts in which the Royal Navy played a very key part. Interestingly, after the Navy, Stephen Morris enjoyed certain comparatively brief stints in other arms of Her Majesty's Armed Forces, and finally recently retired after a distinguished lengthy service in the Metropolitan Police Force.

Having joined the Royal Navy in 1972 and after completing Basic Training and Trade Training at *HMS Raleigh* in Plymouth, Devon, I joined *HMS Hermes*, which had been converted from a fixed wing aircraft Carrier to a Helicopter Commando Carrier. She was always fondly known as the Happy H.

The first deployment was to the Med in 1974. It was during this tour that the Turks and Greeks went at it on the Island of Cyprus, both wanting to claim it as their own. *Hermes* was tasked to assist with the evacuation of British citizens who were caught up in War. The ship used its helicopters and landing craft to pick up the civilians and bring them back to *Hermes* where they were billeted in the various commando mess areas. Members of the ship's company were detailed to look after them on the journey to Gibraltar where they were flown home. Among these were the actor Edward Woodward and his actress wife Michelle Dotrice and, I believe, their children.

As we were "closed up" into Defence Watches at the time because of a possible threat to the ship, we saw very little of the people we had brought on board, but I do know that they were well looked after and were appreciative of our efforts to look after them.

I was tasked with taking a landing craft to the shores to bring off some of the civilians, I think I did at least two trips back and forth, which was quite scary, but to be honest at the time you do not have time to think about the dangers, only getting the job done.

When we left the Med and were heading home to Plymouth we were diverted to look for a fishing boat that had been reported missing off the Norwegian coast, this turned out to be the alleged British spy ship, the *Gaul*. Now one good thing about being on a big ship was that rough weather had little impact on us; however on this occasion the sea was so rough that we lost our sea boat, which was ripped from its davits. We also suffered other damage to the hull of the ship. Sadly the only evidence of the *Gaul* was some wreckage and a life belt. She was lost with all hands.

On our return to Plymouth and after a small refit we took part in various N.A.T.O. exercises some in the Med with runs ashore to Malta and Gibraltar and not so popular exercises up North calling into such exotic places as Scapa Flow, (the "arse-end" of nowhere)!

Between exercises we did enjoy trips to countries on flag-flying visits. We were all reminded to be on our best behaviour and that our mess mates from wartime service did not get to enjoy the high life of peace time.

236

During one trip to the Mediterranean we called into Malta. A Vulcan Bomber was on a routine flight from the UK to Malta Luqa Airport. It made a heavy landing, suffering damage, and took off again and tried to head for sea. It flew over the *Hermes* in Grand Harbour and seemed to blow up in mid air. One civilian, a woman, was killed together with three of the crew from the Vulcan, which crashed on the small town of Zabbar, narrowly missing the local school. As a member of the buffers crash and repair party, we got together all of our equipment, took off from the ship in a Wessex helicopter, and landed in a field close to Zabbar. It took us seven hours to cut up the wing section that had landed in the middle of a small terraced street. We thought it a miracle at the time that so few people were hurt or killed, to this day it is referred to as the "Miracle of Zabbar".

I have been back to Zabbar with my wife whilst on holiday and at the local church there is a small museum with some of the Vulcan wreckage. The people invited me to sign the visitors book and we talked for some time about the events of that day.

Most of the time whilst on exercises at sea we were shadowed by Russian ships called A.G.I.s or Aliens Gathering Intelligence. They were supposed to look like fishing boats but had more aerials and satellite dishes than a council estate in Peckham. When the A.G.I.s were not around we were followed by Russian Bear and Badger aircraft who were seen off by Phantom and Lightning aircraft of the Fleet Air Arm or the RAF.

I have seen some wonderful sights when travelling "up north". We saw sights that I will never forget like the Northern Lights, icebergs, whales. Dolphins swim close to the ship; listening to them singing to each other via the ships sonar. We took the *Hermes* into a deep water fjord; I will never forget that. I am sure people do not believe me when I say we went into a fjord but believe me those waterways are deep. My sister and her husband recently went on a cruise to Scandinavia and they realised just how vast the fjords can be.

Although this was peace time and there were no hostilities, the sea could still be a dangerous place and at times accidents happened and people were hurt and killed. During my time on *Hermes* we had three helicopters that ditched in the sea. Not all of the crew survived.

One dangerous practise was called a R.A.S. or Replenishment at Sea. My job at the time was with the buffers party. This job at sea is all about looking after the rigging and upper deck fittings and seamanship tasks. We also formed part of special sea duty men for entering and leaving harbour. Whilst completing an RAS there are no guard rails in place so you had to be on the ball and at the top of your game; one mistake could lead to fatal consequences.

We also had royalty on board during our deployment to the Americas and the Caribbean. His Royal Highness, Prince Charles, who flew a Wessex helicopter, was on board. I was detailed along with two of my mates to paint his cabin. This we duly did and left a plaque with our names on it stating "By Royal Appointment Painters and Decorators to His Royal Highness the Prince of Wales".

The Americas trip was a mixture of exercises with the American and Canadian Navies and also their land forces. We formed part of a task force that included *H.M.S. Ark Royal* which was filming the television series called "Sailor" which made famous the Rod Stewart song "Sailing". This series was supposed to be a fly-on-the-wall documentary, a tale of every day naval folk. It portrayed the ship in real time, warts and all, which in part was a bit embarrassing for those taking part.

We were lucky to visit many places during the American deployment. We called into different Caribbean Islands, Puerto Rico, Aruba, and Curacao. We laid off Belize for the Royal Marines to exercise and then started a major war games exercise with the Americans as the enemy. This time we won and we even beat them at boxing. I took part as a member of the ships boxing team, and I still have the medal that I won.

After the Caribbean we went to Fort Lauderdale in Florida and took in the sites of Miami, Disneyland and the Everglades. In the Everglades I had one philosophy, if it moved I either killed it or ran away, (I did a lot of running away.)

From there we went to Canada - Halifax, St Johns, Montreal, and Quebec - and then home to England after seven months of "Jolly Jacks" fun and frolics on the high seas. On our return to the UK, *Hermes* went in for a major refit to have the new ski ramp fitted for Sea Harrier Aircraft, and I was drafted to *HMS Galatea*, an anti-submarine frigate, which started another chapter in my life in the Royal Navy.

HMS Galatea was a Leander class Ikara Frigate. The Ikara is a Maori throwing a spear and the anti-submarine missile system was named after this. I was drafted to the ship to gain more experience in anti-submarine warfare. I had passed all of my seamanship exams for Leading Seaman but needed to become more proficient in A/S Warfare.

HMS GALATEA

During this time there was a dispute running between British and Icelandic fisherman over the fishing rights in the North Sea and North Atlantic. This lead to some pretty hostile action by the fisherman on both sides, they would ram each other and cut the warps that held the fishing nets which, when under the stress of full nets, would whip back causing damage and potentially fatal injuries to anyone who was in the way.

It was decided by the British Government to deploy Royal Navy ships to the fishing grounds to protect our fishing fleet and to prevent both sides from the carrying out of dangerous practices that were taking place. This however did not stop the fisherman and the Icelandic vessels started to ram the Royal Navy ships.

Iceland also deployed their own gunboats. Two which I came into contact with were the *Baldur* and *Odin*. These were fast patrol vessels and we were unable to keep up with, or manoeuvre as fast as, them.

Galatea was never damaged although we came close at times, but a number of British warships were and below are some photographs of the type of damage that was caused, and as a result of which led to the Royal Navy ships being reinforced with shaped and cut railway sleepers on the bows and stern and some in the mid-ships region.

THE BASHED IN BOWS OF HMS YARMOUTH

I think it fair to say we were all glad when this was over and although no shots were fired it was dangerous work at sea that focused the mind. On our return I was able to continue with my advancement and passed my Leading Seaman's exams and was rated to Leading Hand.

I was by this time married and we had our young daughter so I was glad of some shore time as a Leading Hand at *HMS Pembroke*, Chatham. I was put to work as an accommodation block Leading Hand in charge of Mountbatten block and my secondary role was L/S in charge of the internal Security Platoon. It was good to have an almost daily routine job going home at the end of each day just like everyone else. My time at Pembroke was broken by two major events. The 1977 Jubilee when we took *HMS Lynx* out of reserve for the Spit Head review during which time I received my first medal. *HMS Lynx* was by that time an old Cat Class Frigate and one of the last Frigates to have twin 4.5inch guns forward and aft.

The Admiral of our flotilla congratulates me on being Rated Leading Hand

HMS Lynx

One Monday in 1978 a buzz went around that *Pembroke* was to be put on a high state of alert. Almost immediately we were ordered to muster or parade at the guard room to draw weapons and put barriers and other security measures in place to close down *Pembroke*. No one in, no one out. Once this was done I was ordered to a briefing where we were told that we were to be used to accommodate the security forces and vehicles for the Arab and Israeli peace talks which were to take place at Leeds Castle in Kent and that this would go on for a possible two weeks and that we were "Watch On, Stop On" – In other words, not going home!

I must say we looked great with our side-arms, sub-machine guns and SLR rifles – a force to be reckoned with, but not a bullet between us. We raised this issue with the Master at Arms who scratched his head and said: "If we give you silly sods bullets, the chances are you'll shoot me". He had a point.

I am glad to say that the peace talks went ahead with no incidents and within the week life went back to normal. Until the fire fighters strike when we were back in action fighting fires. St Mary's Island at Chatham had a fire ground and I believe most military personnel that were to be used in the area were trained at the ground. Prince Phillip visited the fire ground and we manned the Green Goddess Engines until the end of the strike.

I had by this time made up my mind to leave the Navy. It did not suit my wife and although I would have liked to have stayed in "the mob" I decided that they must come first. Having given notice, I was then drafted much to my annoyance to Rosyth in Scotland to an old Tribal Class Frigate, *HMS Eskimo*, although it was rumoured to be coming back to Chatham to pay off. I needed to be as near to home as possible to arrange my life in civvy street. As luck would have it, another lad who lived in Northern Ireland had the reverse problem so we were able to swap our drafts and I ended up on *HMS Achilles* for six months prior to leaving the Navy for civvy street.

I can honestly say that, over all, I enjoyed my time in the Navy. I did and saw things that it would take most people a lifetime to see and achieve. It taught me self discipline and reliance. I made some good mates some of whom I am still in touch with and I would certainly recommend to any young person that they give it a go.

The Tigers' Piper and His Pipes

Murdoch "Mac" MacLeod

Somewhat different from our other accounts, the following story focuses perhaps less on human individuals but rather on the journey of a set of pipes throughout more than a century of assorted warfare and conflict. Mac MacLeod, a member of the RBL Paris branch, has played the lament at the armistice service in Notre Dame Cathedral for a number of years. He contributed this account, adapted from an article by Guy Warner (The Tigers' Piper and His Pipes, Spirit of The Air, Volume 2, Number 5, 2007) and a report by Stewart Mitchell, Volunteer Researcher, the Gordon Highlanders Museum.

It is most unusual, if not unique, for a squadron of the Royal Air Force to have an Honorary Piper and for the piper's bagpipes to be adorned with an OC's Pipe Banner carried on the drones. However, bearing in mind that, for nearly 50 years, 230 Squadron's main role has been to provide air mobility for ground forces, then this may be seen as appropriate and fitting. The bagpipes themselves have a remarkable history, no less inspiring than that of the squadron for which they are played.

Mac was taught to play the pipes by Pipe-Major Alex Taylor who served with the 2nd Battalion, The Gordon Highlanders. Every afternoon during the week for the six years that Alex tutored Murdoch, each lesson finished with stories of the pipes' history.

The pipes, which were made by Henderson in the 1870s, were taken onto the ledger of the Drums and Pipes of the 92nd Regiment of Foot, which in 1881 became the 2nd Battalion, The Gordon Highlanders. In 1880, the 92nd when based on the North West Frontier, took part in the campaign into Afghanistan. In just 23 days, the regiment marched the 320 miles from Kabul to Kandahar, the Drums and Pipes playing most of the way. In the following years, they became masters of colonial warfare in the Sudan, and were (temporarily) turned into sailors, floating up the Nile in an effort to relieve General Charles Gordon (no relation to the Regiment) in Khartoum. In a subsequent battle on the Frontier in 1897, the 1st Battalion's piper, George Findlater, earned the Victoria Cross. Though badly wounded, he propped himself up against a small rock in the middle of intense enemy fire; striking up his pipes he played on to encourage the Gordons on to victory. He was presented with his medal by Queen Victoria in person.

With the commencement of the Boer War in 1899, the 2nd Battalion was posted to South Africa. After initial engagements, it moved to protect the town of Ladysmith, to which the Boers laid siege. When a relief force arrived three months later, they were welcomed by the sound of the 2nd Battalion's Drums and Pipes. The Gordons also took part in the fighting at Magersfontein and Paardeberg (where Major General Hector Macdonald - "Fighting Mac" - commanded the Highland Brigade).

The 2nd Battalion was in Egypt when the Great War broke out. It was hastily recalled and entered Holland in October 1914. It can claim to be one of the very few units to have achieved its objectives on the first day of the Somme, though within three days of fighting there they lost two-thirds of the officers and half the men. As its Battle Honours attest, the Regiment played its part in almost every major action on the Western Front between 1914 and 1918. After the devastation of the Great War, in which 27,000 Gordons were killed or wounded, pipers were no longer permitted to lead troops into battle. The Regiment lost 16 of its 18 pipers in just the first two weeks in France doing precisely that. In subsequent years the Drums and Pipes confirmed their place as valuable operational soldiers, as well as being central to military morale. They performed the role of a machine gun platoon in addition to their normal duties. Piper Harry Lunan, who piped the Gordons through the Great War, survived to be the oldest remaining piper from that war.

This set of pipes, by then tempered on battlefields across the world for more than 50 years, was issued to Alex Taylor, who enlisted on the 16th of December 1935, and completed his basic training in 1936. Alex must have been quite exceptional as, in 1939, he won the annual competition for the "Usher Silver Chanter". The Second World War brought much misfortune for the Gordons; the 1st Battalion was captured at Dunkirk, while a similar fate befell the 2nd Battalion after the Japanese conquest of Singapore, one of whose number was Alex. To escape rotting in Changi Gaol, he accepted the offer to work up jungle on the Death Railway (on the promise of excellent conditions and rations, which was to prove a lie). The Japanese encouraged a piper to form part of a work detail and perhaps it can be said that the sound of the pipes encouraged many a sorely-pressed body and spirit to endure the privations and cruelty. Archive information indicates that Alex was being held in POW "Camp 1", Thailand. However "Camp 1" refers to a work group area rather than a specific place with its HQ at the southern end of the Thai-Burma railway at Nong Pladuk but covering camps up to Tamarkan (where the famous Bridge on the River Kwai was located) some 56 kilometres up the track.

The railway was completed in October 1943 and the majority of the men were moved to other areas, including Japan to work on other projects, such as mining etc. It is understood that Alex travelled to Japan in a hell ship, possibly the *Arimus Maru*, in unspeakable conditions and ended the war in Japan, at Nagoya Number 3 Camp, Funatsu, near to Kobe working in the lead mines.

Alex was liberated in the lead mines in Japan after VJ day. Although emaciated, he was one of the lucky ones, as many of the soldiers from his battalion that marched into captivity didn't survive their cruel ordeal and perished due to the lack of rations, medication and the brutality of the guards, the Koreans being worse than the Japanese. On Alex's return to the UK, the Quartermaster wrote off the pipes from the Regimental ledger, as he took one look at the emaciated piper that stood before him and decided that he deserved to own them.

Alex never charged Mac a penny for tuition, but made him promise that if he ever passed the gift of piping on, it was to be at no cost. He has kept his word. Alex was an excellent teacher; this was evidenced by the fact that Mac won the Scottish Schools' solo competition two years in a row and other competitions (including Pipe Band competitions leading the Pipe Band as Pipe-Major). The first tune a piper normally learns is "Highland Laddie", but Alex taught Mac the "Flowers of the Forest" to highlight the fact that he had played at so many funerals in the Far East. When Alex died prematurely in 1978 at the age of 61, directly as a result of medical conditions brought on by his captivity, Mac was honoured to play the pipes at his funeral with the permission of all of the senior pipers present.

He has played at many since, but notably at the military funeral of Major Matt Titchener, Royal Military Police, who was killed in Iraq in 2003.

He has also played at the White House for President Carter, in St Petersburg, regularly for British Airways and, as a student, was the Scottish Tourist Boards' piper. He has played these pipes in many far-off places, for example in the Arctic, where he followed the route taken by his ancestor on his mother's side, Sir Alexander Mackenzie, the first European to cross the American continent overland to reach the Pacific Ocean.

Lt Col Macleod – Decommissioning former Warsaw Pact missiles – Bosnia

Mac also played the pipes during his military service in B.A.O.R. (British Army of the Rhine), Belgium, France, Kosovo, Naples (AFSOUTH), Northern Ireland, Norway, South America, and on completion of his military service as a Lt Col on operations in Bosnia.

The pipes have flown in an assortment of aircraft including these military types: F16 and SAAB Gripen fighter aircraft; Puma; Lynx, Gazelle; Wessex; Chinook; Sea King and Merlin helicopters, fixed-wing VC10 and

Hercules transport aircraft. In 2003, Mac presented the Squadron with a CO's Pipe Banner (all COs in the Scottish Division have one) which he carries on his pipe drones when playing for the Squadron. One side of the Banner has a tiger skin pattern with the pentagon badge (adopted by the Squadron during the Indonesian Confrontation in the 1960s); the other side has the RAF colours with the Squadron Badge. The banner hangs outside the OC's office and beneath it is a picture of Mac which he finds rather amusing, because the last image that an airman has sight of, is his face before they are marched in front of the OC on orders!

230 (Tiger) Sqn Piper

An Unlikely Hero

Roger Warby

Roger Warby spent the majority of his life working in investment banking and was indeed at the top of his game up to his retirement ten years ago. He however is representative of a class of a generation who missed out on mandatory national service and who always felt he should have provided some time towards the service of his nation. As such, he joined the Territorial Army (Royal Artillery), being paid the "King's Shilling" whilst working in his civilian position in the banking industry.

Having no recollection of WW2 by virtue of being born half-way through it, I then managed also to miss conscription by only reaching the age of 16 when the UK abolished the call-up. Somewhat dissatisfied at having made no military contribution, I joined the Royal Artillery, Territorial Army (i.e. the reserves) as a Gunner in the late 1950s.

Whilst the T.A. had its good points, the overall experience was rather disappointing in that I never got to fire a field gun. This would normally have happened during our annual two-week camps on Salisbury plain, near Devizes. However, at the height of the cold war in the 1960s our leaders decided that it would be more useful to have us practice constructing trench-based nuclear fallout shelters in which we would huddle overnight before emerging the next morning to learn the skills of riot control. Clearly the Army had decided that it would have to manage things (including the UK population) in the event of our suffering nuclear attack.

Eventually I sought and obtained an honourable discharge from HM Armed Forces, which if nothing else qualified me for membership of the Royal British Legion. My wife Janet had also joined the R.B.L., following in her family tradition, and she soon rose to the rank of Committee member and Standard Bearer, Herne Bay branch. This inevitably led to my joining her in the latter capacity as Branch Standard Bearer to her Women's Section Bearer. We attended a number of Standard Bearer training sessions run by the R.B.L. in Aylesford, Kent, where, thanks to the attentions of a number of old but real soldiers, I achieved a level of proficiency not quite on a par with that of Janet, who was for many years Deputy County Bearer for the Kent Women's Section.

Life being largely a series of unrelated accidents, we found ourselves many years later based in Paris where we joined as Standard Bearers one of the oldest R.B.L. branches, founded in 1921 – actually a few months before the foundation of the British Legion itself (the Royal patronage was bestowed some considerable time later). Many impressive and moving ceremonies followed, mostly organised by French institutions but some led by the R.B.L. – notably at the Arc de Triomphe, Notre Dame Cathedral and various locations in the Somme region.

In the late Summer of 1994 we were approached by the staff of HM Ambassador to France, who had accepted the invitation of the City of Amiens and its Mayor and County *Prefet* to attend a day-long event in the city marking its liberation by the British Army 50 years earlier. Amiens was the largest French city liberated by our forces, and invitations had also been accepted by five or six British veterans who had taken part and were still alive and well. The Ambassador naturally required our presence, with our flags.

The day itself was memorable for a number of reasons; together with our French counterparts we carried out various ceremonies of remembrance at diverse memorials in and around the city, culminating in a drive-past by a French armoured column saluting the hundred or so French and British Standards drawn up on either side of the road. We then marched off to a thanksgiving service held in the Cathedral of Amiens, a magnificent edifice and World Heritage site. When the service had finished we repaired to a large marquee, erected adjacent to the Cathedral, for refreshments.

Roger Warby (Parade Marshall) at the Arc de Triomphe, Paris

Accustomed as we were to accepting beer and sandwich fare after R.B.L. ceremonies in the UK, we were most agreeably surprised to find awaiting us canapés, *petits fours* and champagne! The French certainly carry these receptions off with style . . . Speeches inevitably followed, with the *Prefet* and the Mayor of Amiens thanking and lauding their city's liberators whom they were delighted to honour 50 years after their achievement.

The Mayor then said that he wished to award the Medal of Amiens to the distinguished British veterans who had freed the city, and produced a list of names to announce for this purpose. The first name he read out was . . . mine! In a state of some confusion I could only guess that the list of British participants had been drawn up by our Embassy without distinction between veterans and present-day R.B.L. Standard Bearers. The medals were inscribed with the names of the recipients, so for this reason and in order not to bring the proceedings to an embarrassing halt, I accepted the gong with as much grace as I could muster. There followed a presentation of bouquets of Picardy roses to the veterans' wives, and once again the list included an impostor - this time Janet.

As we were recovering from these unexpected and undeserved honours it was announced that lunch would follow in the Town Hall for a select group of participants, namely the *Prefet* and Mayor and their entourages, HM Ambassador and his staff and the British veterans and wives, including Janet and myself as British Standard Bearers. Lunch was a very convivial and agreeable occasion, but for me nemesis was at hand in the form of a young reporter for the local newspaper who approached me at the end of the meal to enquire as to my recollections of the day we liberated Amiens! After nearly choking on my wine – and resolving to die my hair for future functions of this type, I managed to stutter that it was difficult for me to recall the day in detail having been so young at the time . . . I did not elaborate on this to reveal that I was in fact two years old!

Despite this comical end to what had been a splendid day, it turned out that my response to the reporter was not so different from what the real heroes told me later – that they had little recollection of the Amiens liberation since they left within 24 hours to go on to Lille and then Belgium, where they liberated Brussels and Antwerp. In fact many of them and their comrades finished up in Holland where they were involved in Operation Market Garden and its bridge too far.

Their valour and subsequent modest recounting of their exploits mark them out as heroes indeed, and it was a privilege for me to be – mistakenly – identified as one of them.

Amiens Medal, presented to Roger Warby, 28th August, 1994

My Involvement with the Royal British Legion and the Wonderful People I have Met

Janet Warby

Janet Warby has been heavily involved with the work of the Royal British Legion for over 25 years; she has been a key supporter of this work, and it seems only fitting that her story should be in this book. In many ways, she forms some of the glue that has helped unite all of these stories into one piece of work.

I have been involved with The Royal British Legion since I was 16 years old. My grandmother enrolled me into her Women's Section unknown to me at the time. I always watched the BBC broadcast of The Festival of Remembrance at The Royal Albert Hall, and marvelled at the many Standard Bearers, my grandmother being one of them.

Some years later, my family came back to UK after living in Belgium and France. We had become used to taking our two children to the various bars and cafes on the Continent, so to continue being able to go out as a family, we joined the R.B.L. in Herne Bay, Kent. My father, being ex-RAF, was a member and my husband, Roger, having been in the Royal Artillery, T.A., was also eligible to join as an Ordinary Member. This type of membership changed some years later.

My mother had joined the Women's Section and as numbers were low asked me if I would like to join. I immediately signed on. After about four months, I became the Deputy Standard Bearer for the Women's Section. I then had to take on the full role when the then current Standard Bearer developed back problems. I decided I needed to be trained properly and joined in one of the Training Days at Aylesford near the Royal British Legion Village. These were arranged by two of the Parade Marshals who would put us through our paces on parade. It was hard work learning all the different movements that we had to do with the Standard but it was also fun. Everyone looked out for each other.

The first time I entered the County Competition was in the Novice Cup where, I came second. I was very pleased with this as I had only been the Standard Bearer for a short while. Next time I entered the competition – I could not be called a novice anymore – I came second again and became the Deputy County Standard Bearer, Women's Section, for Kent. What an honour this was - occasionally I had to carry the Union Flag. By this time I had also become Secretary of my Women's Section in Herne Bay. Just before I was due to leave Kent to come to France for a second time, I was asked if I would consider putting my name forward for Kent County Secretary. I would have loved to do this but we were on the move again.

This was 1992. We moved back to France and quickly found the Paris Branch of the R.B.L. Somehow they found out that both Roger and I had previous experience in the Legion and so we very quickly found ourselves as Standard Bearer's and on the Committee.

My first French parade was by invitation to one of the French *Anciens Combatants* Associations. I was asked by my then Chairman, John Gardner, if I would attend this ceremony. So having made sure my uniform was pressed, nice white ironed shirt, Standard cleaned and the brasses gleaming, hair not on my collar, I set off for the Arc de Triomphe.

I was scared stiff and wondered what I had got myself into. I need not have worried, as a kind little lady, carrying the Free French flag, came up to me and started to talk to me in English. She introduced herself as Paulette Levalleur and said she had been in London with General Charles de Gaulle during the war. I immediately warmed to her and we have become firm friends. Paulette introduced me to several of the other Standard Bearers, one of whom was Fred Canncelloni, originally from Italy – you could tell by the surname – but who had become a French citizen. Fred was a scream; he told many stories of how as a young man, he had worked with the Americans as a guide, interpreter and anything they wanted him to be. He always told his stories with a smile. Fred said that when the Americans pulled out of the South of France, they took Fred with them; to have left him behind would have been folly since, if the Germans caught him, they would have shot him as a spy. Fred became a Vice-President and Standard Bearer for the American Legion in Paris.

On one occasion at the Arc de Triomphe, we were waiting to be called to attention, when the eagle, on the top of the pole with the Stars and Stripes, fell off. I took one look and said "Fred, the Eagle has landed". Everyone roared with laughter. I had not realised what I had said until they all started to laugh. Thankfully Fred saw the funny side of my comment.

Apart from Paulette and Fred, I have met many brave and amusing people, who like us, carry the Standard of their associations. Roger and I became quite close to a Jewish couple called Anisten. Janine Anisten was the Standard Bearer for the Jewish Association, where her husband was the Chairman. Mr. Anisten had been rounded up with other Jewish boys during the war and sent by train to a Concentration Camp. On route, the train stopped, the door of his wagon was not shut properly and so with a couple of the other boys, he escaped into a farmer's field where there were big bales of hay. The farmer and his wife took the boys in and looked after them until it was safe for them to get back to Paris. He survived the war thanks largely to the kind farmer and his wife.

These are just a few of the stories I can remember. Fred and Mr. Anisten are no longer with us but Paulette is a member of the Paris Branch of the Legion and until quite recently, she and her late husband, Roger, carried their respective flags at our events. Paulette is 92 years of age.

The Royal British Legion, Paris Branch, was given the honour of re-kindling the flame at the Arc de Triomphe on 4th August in 1924. This was the day Britain and her dominions entered World War I. On 11th November, 1924, we were also given the privilege of holding a Service of Remembrance at the Cathedral of Notre Dame de Paris. We still do these ceremonies to date, the one at Notre Dame, is in the presence of H.M. Ambassador to France, Commonwealth Ambassadors, Attachés, French VIPs, British Community Members and our French counterparts. We also have a Piper and Bugler present. The 4th August also has a Commonwealth theme, as we ask a Commonwealth Ambassador in rota to re-kindle the flame on behalf of Her Majesty, the UK and Commonwealth. Both are moving ceremonies.

One year, we were low on Standard Bearers, owing to age and some moving away from Paris. I met a lady called Pauline Harrison in the Legion, who had come to join as she was new in Paris and was in the T.A. of Queen Alexandra's Royal Army Nursing Corps. Pauline had been sent out to the Gulf in the first of the wars in that area. She was a Nursing Sister in her civilian life. So she worked in the hospital in the Gulf. One of her jobs was to teach the American GIs how to get into

Janet Warby on parade, carrying the Union Jack, at Notre Dame

their Bio-Chemical suits in well under a minute. She said that had the drill been for real many of them would have been dead since they were so slow.

I asked Pauline if she fancied carrying a Standard with me. She agreed but did not know what to do, so I suggested that she come to my home; I would show her and we could practice together. After several sessions, she got the idea and we were all set. She came to me one day and said that as she was in the QAs, perhaps she should carry the Union Flag. I said I had no objection to this, but questioned her as to whether she realised that all the other Standard Bearers would take their moves from her? With this in mind she promptly replied: "You do it"! We had some laughs together and to be honest I am not sure how we did not get drummed out of the 'brownies' as we used to call it. We used to put the Piper and Bugler up in a hotel. We would meet them at the Legion on the day of the Notre Dame Ceremony and then take them to the Cathedral. One day Pauline was looking at their shoes and admiring the shine. She asked them how they got them to shine as well as they did. They told her how, but she said she could not get her shoes like theirs. Next thing I knew, she had her shoes out of the bag and gave them one each and asked them to shine her shoes for her! I don't know how she did it, but I had to laugh at her. We are still friends to this day, although we do not see each other that much as she is in the UK and I am still here in Paris.

The Cold War, 1945-1989

Roger Thorn

When in 1989 the West German Army Chief-of-Staff had access to the east German Army Staff files the world learnt for the first time officially that the Warsaw Pact battle plan provided for an attack on the NATO forces at a moment of their own choosing, and not necessarily at a moment of provocation or of heightened political tension.

32 years earlier, snow was lying thick on the ground in the winter of 1957 on the East German border. It was just as well that we British soldiers did not know the Warsaw Pact's intentions. We were well aware of their presence. If we had read "War and Peace" we would have been able to recall that electric moment when the enemy troops were first seen moving along on the opposite side of the valley. It is true that the West had known only 12 years of peace since VE Day in 1945.

In May 1957 I had passed out at a Commissioning Parade as a National Service officer after basic training in Catterick and Officer training at Mons Officer Cadet School. I had been posted to a Regiment in B.A.O.R. on the East German border. After my drafting leave, on my way to the station at the start of my journey I had decided to call on my mother's elder sister, a widow living in the family house where she and her two brothers and three sisters had grown up. On the phone she had sounded enthusiastic, but when I arrived in uniform she burst into tears, which for me as a 19 year old was rather embarrassing, and difficult to cope with. However she gathered herself quite quickly and immediately apologized. "You see", she explained "the last time I saw a soldier's uniform in this house was exactly 40 years ago, when my two elder brothers Thomas and Harold, left at the end of their very short leave in England before going back to the Western front in the summer of 1917. I last saw them go out of the door you have just come through".

They never returned – that much I already knew; they were both killed at Passchendaele the following winter. Seeing me in khaki battledress had suddenly brought it all back to my Aunt, and here was I now just about to go back out through the same door as them. It turned out to be my final farewell to her in the event, because she died six months later. I felt a pang of guilt for not having foreseen the emotional shock which she must have experienced.

Thomas served in The Royal Warwickshire Regiment, where he would have encountered a certain Lt. Bernard Montgomery, who was shot in a lung at Passchendaele, but survived. Thomas is buried at the Cement House Cemetery near Ypres, and I last visited his grave when the RBL Paris Branch organized a visit to the battlefields around Ypres. When walking slowly over the open ground leading to the village of Passchendaele, our guide Colonel Oliver Warman, turned to me at one point and said "Your uncle would have been killed about here" and we stopped briefly. On the same tour we visited Tyne Cot and I saw Harold's name on the memorial there. He had served in The Wiltshire Regiment.

Youth has its own survival mechanisms so that I was not too concerned on arriving at my unit to be told that the nearest Warsaw Pact tanks were only 40 kilometres away. As with all peacetime armies the challenge was to keep the men occupied both on and off duty. Drill and kit inspections were frequent, and often carried out with little notice. Morning parades were however daily and it fell to the Orderly Officer to conduct the inspection with the Orderly Sergeant. I have a clear memory of marching over one morning with Sergeant M[1] to the Vehicle Park where the drivers of Austin Champs and of Three-ton lorries were lined up for inspection, many of them newly posted to the Regiment and therefore unknown to me or the Sergeant. Sergeant M was an Irishman whose tongue was permanently green, not as a show of patriotism, but because his favourite poison was Crème de Menthe.

On arrival in front of the drivers I was saluted by the Orderly Corporal. He followed us silently as we inspected the front rank. The drivers were in work denims, but had clean webbing, brasses, cap-badge and boots. Stopping in front of one driver the Sergeant bellowed: "You're dressed like a sack of potatoes!" It was true. It was hard to imagine a less military bearing. His equipment was "eye-maculate", as we had learnt to say in basic training, but his denims hung about him. They went well however with his hang-dog expression, as he looked at us with a pale oval face and drooping, sad eyes. He had hunched shoulders and I wondered how on earth he had managed to impress his driving instructors at Ripon with any sense of alertness, "a sense of urgency" as the Army called it. He was clearly not happy in uniform.

"What's your name, Driver?" barked the Sergeant. "Driver Banks, Sergeant!". "You've lost it!" said the Sergeant, which was the Army's way of saying that he would be on C.O.'s parade the next morning, with no hope of escaping some form of punishment for slovenly

---

1   The full name of the Sergeant is deliberately omitted.

dress. "Take his name, Corporal!" was the Sergeant's next bark.

Before we moved on I said to Driver Banks that he looked unfit and that I would put his name down for an intensive P.T. course.

"I'm not allowed to, Sir," he replied.

"Flat feet?" barked the Sergeant.

"I can't," insisted the hapless driver.

"Don't play games with me," responded the Sergeant, "You'll do as the officer says."

"I mean I can't do sport here," appealed the driver.

"Your feet won't touch the ground," was the next bark.

At this point the silent Orderly Corporal piped up .

"He's right, Sergeant. He flies back every weekend to play football."

"What's your first name, Driver Banks?" I offered.

"Gordon, Sir."

We were inspecting Driver Gordon Banks (Chesterfield F.C., and later Leicester City, Stoke City and England Goalkeeper).

If you're old enough, do you remember his "Save of the Century" against Pele in the 1970 World Cup?

About the Editor

Grahame Warby lives and works in the City of London. After having worked in legal private practice for seven and a half years and then a year working as General Counsel (in-house) for a leading Egyptian steel manufacturer, he now recruits lawyers throughout Europe and the Far East for private practice.

Grahame was educated and lived in his formative years in Paris and then returned to the UK in 1996 to undertake four years of university study where he gained a BA (Hons) degree in Law with History, and a Masters degree (LL.M) in Public and Private International Law. He has published over 30 articles and one other book in the last 12 years.

Grahame can be reached at grahamewarby@yahoo.co.uk

Index